INSIGHT COMPACT GUIDES

Ba

GREAT LITTLE GUIDES

Compact Guide: Bali shows you where you can still find the magic on this enchanting island despite the boom in tourism. It sets out comprehensive itineraries, provides useful tips and gives valuable insights into the religious and cultural life of the Balinese.

This is just one title in *Apa Publications'* new series of pocket-sized, easy-to-use guidebooks intended for the independent-minded traveller. *Compact Guides* pride themselves on being up-to-date and authoritative. They are in essence mini travel encyclopedias, designed to be comprehensive yet portable, as well as readable and reliable.

Star Attractions

An instant reference to some of Bali's most popular tourist attractions to help you on your way.

Ubud p25

Nasa Dua p21

Pura Tanah Lot p35

Batubulan p36

Gianyar p43

Pura Besakih p45

Terracing p53

Pura Kehen p58

Gamelan player

Gunung Batur p60

Lombok p63

Bali

Introduction

Bali – Island of Gods and Demons 5
Historical Highlights...16

Places

Route 1: The South: Kuta/Legian – Sanur and Nusa Dusa........**20**
Route 2: Ubud and environs...**25**
Route 3: Temples of mountain and sea: Mengwi – Marga –
Gunung Batukau – Pura Luhur – Tanah Lot **32**
Route 4: The Craftsmen's Road: Batubulan – Celuk – Mas –
Peliatan – Ubud **36**
Route 5: Bali's oldest shrines: Ubud – Tampaksiring –
Gunung Kawi – Pejeng – Yeh Pulu – Goa Gajah **38**
Route 6: To the Mother Temple: Gianyar – Klungkung –
Pura Besakih – Putung – Candi Dasa........................**43**
Route 7: The North Coast: Candi Dasa – Amed – Tulamben –
Kubutambahan – Singaraja – Lovina Beach **53**
Route 8: Baroque temples and austere scenery: Sidan –
Gunung Batur – Jagaraga – Singaraja – Lovina..........**58**
Route 9: The rice terraces of Pupuan: Lovina Beach –
Pupuan – Antosari – South Bali **62**
Route 10: Lombok **63**

Culture

Temples **69**
Festivals and Ceremonies **71**
Balinese Art **73**
Music, Theatre and Dance **76**

Leisure

Food and Drink **81**
Active Holidays **85**

Practical Information

Getting There..**89**
Getting Around **90**
Facts for the Visitor..**92**
Accommodation...**98**

Index **104**

Bali – Island of Gods and Demons

Rangda and Barong, the Balinese personifications of black and white magic, pit their individual strengths against each other. It is a desperate struggle, where each is fighting to gain the upper hand. And yet, the Balinese know that neither of them will win. The ancient rivalry represented in this drama is more than just a competition or an absorbing form of entertainment. It represents a microcosm of the world at large where good maintains a shaky equilibrium with evil, each striving to outdo the other.

Warding off evil

Many visitors arrive with the notion that on Bali they will find one of the world's last paradises. Intoxicated by the lilting sounds of a gamelan orchestra and the heady scent of incense sticks, a good number are lulled into believing that they have. It is an image which survives despite the apocalypse of Kuta with its half-naked sun-worshippers, importunate traders, marauding massage women, fast-food restaurants and ear-splitting discotheques.

Maintaining traditions

With hordes of people visiting the 'Island of the Gods' every year, one might ask how long it will be before the rice farmers stop placing their faith in the power of Dewi Sri, the goddess of the rice harvest, and transfer their allegiance to artificial fertilisers. How much longer will the Balinese continue to devote more time to their gods and demons than to their mortal resort hotel employers and the pursuit of financial gain? Bali has opened its doors to Western culture and is currently walking the tightrope between modernity and tradition.

Today, the struggle between Rangda and Barong still ends in a draw, and the island's gods and demons and its rich cultural legacy, exist alongside high technology and mass tourism. For the moment at least, the Balinese cosmos still is in harmony with itself. An elaborate purification ceremony takes place on Kuta and other beaches each year, cleansing the island of the year's misdeeds and praying that Bali and its people may continue to resist the winds of change in the years to come. Even the presence of hundreds of gawking, camera-clicking tourists cannot defile this ancient cathartic ritual. And it is all too easy to believe that the power of the gods will prevail over that of mere mortals, at least in the coming year.

Modern influences

Location and landscape

Bali is the westernmost island in the chain that makes up the Lesser Sundas group. It covers 5,600sq km (2,021sq miles), which makes it one of the smallest provinces of the Indonesian archipelago, the largest in the world. Indonesia's 17,508 islands stretch from the Pacific to the Indian Ocean, lying on both sides of the equator between the Malay Peninsula and New Guinea. Lying 8° south of the

5

equator and 115° east of Greenwich, Bali is separated to the west from neighbouring Java by a narrow strip of sea. The Strait of Lombok, which divides Bali from the island of Lombok to the east, is not only considerably wider (30km/19 miles) but also much deeper. In the 19th century, the geographer-scientist Alfred Wallace established that there were marked differences of both vegetation and animal life between Bali and Lombok. The large mammals of western Indonesia, from tiger and rhinoceros to elephants, gave way to marsupials and a number of bird species which were otherwise found only in Australia. From this, Wallace concluded that, 100 million years ago, the Strait of Lombok represented the dividing line between the Asian and Australian continents. The division is known to this day as the Wallace Line.

A chain of volcanoes runs through the islands of Sumatra and Java and continues into Bali, forming Gunung Agung (3,142m/10,308ft), the island's highest mountain, and Gunung Batur (1,717m/5,633ft). The islanders believe these volcanoes to be the abode of the gods, who in their taciturn manner, bless the island with mineral-rich volcanic ash for bountiful harvests but yet remain a permanent threat – the last major eruptions occurred as recently as the 1960s – when the people angered the gods. Also of volcanic origin are the mountain lakes, of which the largest are Lake Batur and Lake Bratan. These lakes feed the rivers which flow through central and southern Bali and provide the water for the irrigation of rice fields.

Despite its size, Bali offers an astonishing variety of landscapes. The southern part of the island, the most fertile region, is characterised by luxuriant tropical vegetation. In the centre lie the misty cloud-covered highlands.

6

Lakes Buyan and Tamblingan, and Bukit Badung Peninsula

The emerald green rice terraces found in the south-central region are irrigated by the waters from mountain lakes and rivers. The Bukit Badung peninsula in the extreme south, on the other hand, is very arid. The northern beaches are formed out of black lava while the west is largely covered with impenetrable jungle. The east coast, by contrast, is largely dry and inhospitable.

Climate

Bali's climate is determined by the monsoon winds and consists of two seasons. During the wet season between November and March the northwest monsoon brings rain and humidity which can be as high as 95 percent. The dry season from May until October is the most pleasant time to visit. Since the island lies virtually on the equator, daytime temperatures climb to about 30°C (86°F) almost every day, although the mountains tend to be about 10°C (18°F) cooler and may even seem chilly at night. The European summer months are definitely the best time to visit Bali, which explains why July and August are high season on the island. Fewer tourists arrive during the European winter, except for Christmas, which is the summer holiday season for Australians. During these months you should not forget to take an umbrella, although you will seldom experience a day of continuous rain, and several wet days at a stretch are a rare occurrence.

An outrigger needs fair winds

7

Nature and environment

Rice farming is an important activity, and the countryside is characterised by a series of artistically laid-out rice terraces (*sawahs*). When ripe, the golden yellow grains sway in the breeze, caressed by Dewi Sri, the Balinese goddess of fertility whose shrine, laden with offerings, is found in a corner of every field. Side by side with the dry fields ready for harvest are freshly flooded emerald green paddies containing young seedlings, and just around the next corner you may come across a farmer ploughing the land with his team of oxen. Bali's countryside is largely determined by its year-round rice-farming culture.

Depending on the variety of rice grown, a period of three to six months will elapse between sowing and harvesting. The seedlings take root initially in seed beds before being transplanted into the irrigated fields where they must be kept immersed in water during the entire period of growth until the rice is ready for harvesting. The water from streams and rivers is diverted to the fields via channels cut into the soft volcanic rock. Thanks to its fertile soil and an irrigation system perfected over centuries, a Balinese farmer can harvest two to three crops a year.

A co-operative (*subak*) ensures that the water is fairly distributed to the fields and that the dams are properly

Rice paddies near Pupuan

Harvest time

maintained. Shortly before harvest time the fields are drained and the women of the neighbourhood congregate to cut the rice stalk by stalk using a small knife called the *ani-ani*, hiding the blade in their hands in order not to frighten Dewi Sri. Today, this traditional method of harvesting the grain is used only for Balinese rice and not for other Indonesian varieties.

Progress ignores religious sentiments, and since the 1970s President Suharto's 'Green Revolution' has propagated new types of high-yield rice which have largely been responsible for making Indonesia self-sufficient in rice production. Recently, however, it has been discovered that these new varieties rapidly exhaust the soil. As a result, Balinese farmers are returning increasingly to the traditional Balinese rice varieties. Not only are they ecologically friendly but they also taste better, as the Balinese point out with a smile.

Ploughing the old way

Other important crops include coconuts, coffee, peanuts, spices such as cloves, cinnamon and vanilla, and tropical fruits such as bananas, pineapples, papayas and mangoes, as well as vegetables. The local wine (*anggur*) production in the north of the island is declining because of the poor quality of the grapes.

Flora and fauna

Bali has been compared to a tropical garden because of the wide variety of plants which flourish there. There are various species of palm tree, bamboo groves, and flowering trees and shrubs like frangipani, poinsettia, bougainvillea and a profusion of orchids. The focal point of most

Bougainvillea
Banyan tree

villages is the banyan tree (*ficus bengalensis*), with its typical aerial roots. The dry Bukit Badung peninsula also is home to the pandanus (screw-pine) and even cacti. Mangrove swamps fringe the coast between Sanur and Nusa Dua and throughout the northwest. Tropical rainforests, which once covered the island, are still found in the west.

Many of them lie within the Bali Barat National Park. This is Bali's 'Wild West', where until a few decades ago you could still find the island's last remaining tigers, rhinoceroses and crocodiles. The park covers an area of 700sq km (253sq miles) and is a paradise for ornithologists. It is one of the last habitats of the Bali starling, also known as the Rothschild mynah bird, a species threatened with extinction. With luck and patience, visitors to the park will be able to see several species of deer and monkey as well as the endangered wild Javan buffalo (*Bos javanicus*).

Of the large mammal species once found on Bali, only the wild boar and deer remain. Monkeys are common and some forests, such as Alas Kedaton, are inhabited by colonies of macaques. Lizards are also found everywhere, including the insect-eating geckos which serve a useful function in many hotel rooms. Snakes, too, are also commonplace. The most important domestic animals are the sway-back pig and the pretty doe-faced Balinese cow, as well as chickens and ducks.

A man's best friend

Population
Bali's present population of some 2.9 million inhabitants can trace their ancestry to the various ethnic groups which migrated to the island from southern China between 2500 and 1500BC. The population density of 510 inhabitants per sq km (1,396 per sq mile) is much greater than that, say, of the United Kingdom (232 inhabitants per sq km). The capital and largest city, Denpasar, has a population of 370,000, with more than 85 percent of the population still living in the rural areas. Bali's annual population growth rate is 1.6 percent and average life expectancy is 68 years.

Most Balinese live in the country

The Hindu-Dharma religion
'Life is Religion, and Religion is Life' – it is no accident that Bali is known as the 'Island of Gods and Demons'. Religion permeates every aspect of everyday life. The daily offerings of food to ancestors and spirits, a cock fight at the beginning of a temple festival or the graceful dance of a young girl all are expressions of a deep religious conviction. The fascination of Balinese culture lies not least in the colourful and sensuous rituals through which the gods are worshipped.

9

Bali and West Lombok form together an enclave of Hinduism in the midst of the largest Muslim country in the world. But the Balinese version of the religion is very different from that practised on the Indian subcontinent.

Hinduism and Buddhism were introduced to Indonesia via Java by traders between the 8th and 16th centuries. The Javanese in turn adopted elements of both religions and incorporated them into indigenous religious practices. This Javanese form of Hinduism arrived in Bali during the 10th century when a Javanese princess married a Balinese king. During the 16th century, when the threat of a Muslim invasion became imminent in Java, the nobles of the Majapahit kingdom, the last great Hindu dynasty on Java, sought refuge on Bali.

Cockfights are part of the religious tradition

Over time, this hybrid Hindu faith developed further, incorporating ancient animist beliefs in spirits and the practice of the ancestor worship handed down through the generations. Today, 94 percent of the population follows this belief, known as Hindu-Dharma or Agama Hindu.

Paying honour to sacred ancestors, deities, spirits and demons can be traced back to pre-Hindu times, as can exorcist practices such as trance dances or sacrifices to appease bad spirits. Equally ancient is the Balinese study

Shiva resides in the mountains

Offerings at Gunung Kawi

Shadows at play

of cosmology, an understanding of which is essential to any comprehension of the Hindu-Dharma religion. The countless daily rituals that the Balinese observe mostly serve to ensure that human existence is in harmony with the cosmos and its divine principles. The Balinese perceive their island as a macrocosm, in which the mountains and space above represent *kaja*, the realm of the gods, while the earth and the space beneath, i.e. the sea, represent *kelod*, the home of the dark powers. The holy mountain Gunung Agung is the residence of the god Shiva and is therefore regarded as the centre of the universe. Man lives in the middle kingdom between these two extremes, and the roads linking the villages, farmsteads and family temples are all aligned along an imaginary axis between the mountain and the sea. *Kaja* and *kelod*, however, also represent in general the contradictory nature of all beings. Heaven and earth, sun and moon, man and woman, life and death, stand in opposition to each other, for the one cannot exist without the other.

Since the world of man lies between the cosmic poles, it is the duty of the Balinese to preserve the harmony. And so they worship gods and demons in equal measure, as can be seen from the small offerings which Balinese women prepare each day with painstaking attention to detail. They are offered to the sacred ancestors in the family temple, to the demons which inhabit the doorstep or at dangerous road intersections, or to the goddess of the rice harvest, Dewi Sri, at the little shrines in the rice fields.

The Balinese have adopted the Hindu belief that every human being is subject to the cycle of reincarnation. For pious Hindus, much worse than death itself is the fact that they must live through an infinite number of existences until they are released. In contrast to Indian Hindus, the Balinese believe that they will be reincarnated within their own clan. The level of reincarnation is determined by *karma*, the sum of all good and evil deeds which go to make up a life. A Hindu's goal is to be liberated from the cycle of reincarnation by living as virtuous a life as possible. Thus, the individual immortal soul will be united with the highest divine principle (*moksha*).

Apart from the Indian social order and their philosophy, the Indian traders also brought with them their mythology, their pantheon of gods, as well as the two epics the *Ramayana* and the *Mahabharata*. These provide the themes for shadow puppet plays and various dance dramas.

The trinity of the highest Hindu deities (*trimurti* or *trisakti*) consists of Brahma, the creator, Vishnu, the preserver, and Shiva, the destroyer and renewer. In temples you often will notice their symbolic colours (red for Brahma, black for Vishnu and white for Shiva). Dewi Sri, the guardian of fertility in general and of rice farming in particular, and Dewi Lakshmi, responsible for happiness and prosperity, are the wives of Vishnu. Dewi Saraswati, Brahma's wife, is greatly revered as the goddess of education and learning. Finally, Shiva's consort Parvati appears in various manifestations – as Durga, the goddess of death, as well as Uma, the goddess of love. In addition, there is an almost infinite list of other deities. All gods, however, are but manifestations of one and the same god – Sang Hyang Widi Wasa, the divine principle.

One manifestation of the same god

You will seldom come across a portrait of Sang Hyang Widi Wasa. Some farmers do not even know the name of the Almighty, instead they will worship various aspects of his nature. Whether Dewi Sri is one goddess amongst many or the manifestation of another great god is of no real significance in everyday religion. All the more important, on the other hand, are such details for the integration of Balinese Hinduism into the Indonesian constitution. The first principle of the *pancasila* order (*see page 15*) states that a religion can only be recognised as such if it provides for a supreme deity, regardless of whether its name is God, Allah, Buddha or Sang Hyang Widi Wasa.

Buddha at Brahma Vihara

For a long time, as in India, its country of origin, Buddhism also was an important religious element. In Bali today, Buddha has acquired the position of a minor Hindu deity, a protective spirit guarding the home. Some priests, however, continue to follow his teachings. They describe themselves as *pedanda boda* as opposed to the *pedanda shiva* priests who serve the Hindu god.

Life for the Balinese would be paradise on earth if they were simply under the protection of their gods and ancestors. However, they have to contend with the powers of darkness, which rule on moonless nights. The land is haunted, in particular, by the *leyaks*, the disembodied souls of the dead who during their lifetime followed the principles of black magic and who are likely to play tricks on the living if they are not adequately appeased.

Temple priest

Religious life on the island centres on sacrifices and purification ceremonies. Offerings consist of anything from a grain of rice to elaborately decorative food. Animals often are sacrificed during a temple festival, and they may be provided by any faithful member of the community. Purification ceremonies, on the other hand, can only take place with the assistance of a priest. He serves as a go-between for man and the gods. The greatest respect is reserved for the pedanda, or high priest, who is a member of the Brahman caste (*see page 12*) and who knows how to sanctify water for the ceremony. He supervises important ceremonies and spends the rest of his life meditating and studying religious texts and rituals. The daily duties in the temple, on the other hand – supervising temple festivals, distributing holy water and directing processions – is the task of the *pemangku*, the assistant priest. This job is not linked to any particular caste.

The caste system and community

The spread of the Hindu religion at the beginning of the 16th century was resisted by the Bali Aga, the original pre-Hindu inhabitants of the island, who still live in a handful of remote villages (*see Tenganan, page 51*). The Hindu caste system was introduced by the Javanese Majapahit kingdom which invaded Bali in the 15th century. There are four castes, each associated with a title which indicates the caste the individual belongs to.

Brahmanas, or priests, form the top caste in Balinese society. Members of this caste are known as Ida Bagu (man) and Ida Ayu (woman). The next caste, the *Kesatria*, comprises the high nobility which once ruled the island, and are distinguished by titles like Anak Agung, Dewa and Cokorde. The *Wesia* form the lower nobility, go by the title of Gusti. Only 3 percent of all Balinese belong to one of these castes, which together are known as Triwangsa. Most Balinese are **Sudra** or **Jaba**, literally the outsiders of the court. Unlike India, there are no lower caste untouchables on the island.

The family, particularly the extended family, forms the basis of social life. In Indonesia, as in other southeast Asian countries, it replaces the national network of social security and retirement pensions found in Western countries. The interests of the family as a whole take precedence over the rights of the individual rights. A typical family home is laid out according to the rules of *kelod-kaja (see page 10)*, with the sleeping and living areas on the mountain side and the work rooms and stalls facing towards the sea. The complex is closed off from prying

12

eyes by a wall, with a small free-standing wall just behind the entrance to prevent demons getting in. The individual buildings and the *bale* (open pavilions) are grouped around the inner courtyard. One of these is the family pavilion in which rites of passage (*see page 71–2*) are celebrated. Holding pride of place are the shrines of the family and ancestors, the most sacred place of all and the scene of daily prayers and offerings.

Despite the unmistakable influence of media and tourism, the lifestyle of the younger generation of Balinese still is governed to a remarkable degree by the traditions which form the basis for an intact family and village community. Most people still are employed in farming and the importance of agriculture can be seen in the predominantly rural-based social structures which prevail on the island to this day. About 85 percent of the population live in a village community, comprising individual village units known as the *banjar*. All adult male family members, who are members of this council, decide on matters of local importance, from minor road repairs to matters such as land rent, the preparation of temple festivals and the maintenance or construction of new temples. The *banjar* also functions as an informal local court. When dealing with disputes it will attempt to arrive at a compromise – usually with success. The *banjar* determines to a large extent how village life functions and its success is due, in part, to the strong Balinese sense of community.

This is amply demonstrated in the *subak* (irrigation co-operative), an association of rice farmers who organise and co-ordinate the essential tasks relating to the irrigation of the rice fields. The *subak* also is responsible for deciding when the fields should be flooded, for the division of work amongst the farmers who share a common irrigation channel, and when the crop is to be harvested. In addition, it also determines the appropriate offerings to the rice goddess Dewi Sri in the *subak* temples, without which no harvest can be successful.

Family shrines

Rice is farmed co-operatively

Language

Bahasa Indonesia is the official language spoken by more than 350 ethnic groups scattered across the geographically and culturally diverse region covered by the Indonesian archipelago. Although Bahasa Indonesia is the working language in schools and the civil service in Bali and is widely spoken, the mother tongue of the people is Balinese. This is in turn divided into two separate versions: High Balinese and Low Balinese.

If you want to win the affection of your hosts quickly, it is well worth trying to learn a little Indonesian. It is not a difficult language. The grammar is easy, as Bahasa Indonesia does not distinguish between gender, nor do its verbs have tenses. Plurals are easily formed, and the rules governing word order within the sentence are flexible. The following is a brief guide to pronunciation of Bahasa Indonesia:

c   mostly 'ch', e.g. *candi* ('chandi' = funeral temple)

j   as in English 'j', e.g. *jalan* ('jalan' = street)

y   as 'ya', e.g. *saya* ('saya' = I)

r   'r' is rolled

s   as 'ss'

h   final 'h' at the end of a syllable is pronounced with an audible expiration of air.

e   is usually pronounced 'ay', e.g. *besok* ('baeysok' = tomorrow) or swallowed between two consonants, e.g. *berapa* ('brapa' = how much).

Economy

Over 75 percent of Bali's population is involved in agriculture. Rice is by far the most important crop, most of it grown for home consumption. In the cooler mountain regions coffee also is grown, as are cloves, fruit, vegetables, maize and coconut palms. Copra, the white flesh of the coconut, is an important export commodity. Fishing and salt extraction have been practised for many years. A new addition is the farming of shrimp in saltwater basins along the coast.

Salt is an important commodity

Tourism has long been the principal source of foreign exchange. Many rice farmers add to their income by letting rooms to tourists, or by producing or selling souvenirs. However, most of the money earned from tourism remains with the international tour operators and hotel chains.

The island's only industry of note is clothing manufacture. Cheap to sophisticated fashions mostly created to suit Western tastes by designers from industrialised countries, is sewn by Balinese women – often as a cottage industry – and sold on the island or exported.

Textile is a cottage industry

During the 1930s, no more than 100 foreigners would arrive on Bali in a month. During the late 1960s and the 1970s, the island was regarded by hippies as the last remaining paradise on earth. Today, mass tourism is essential to the economy. Since the end of the 1980s Bali has enjoyed a tourist boom and the expansion of hotel accommodation, which totals 31,348 rooms in all price categories, seems set to continue. The number of holiday-makers is hovering around 1.4 million a year.

Bali has long been open to Western influence, and the dichotomy between the traditional and modern worlds is very much in evidence. Work in the rice fields, formerly taken for granted, is becoming less important as tourism becomes an increasingly attractive prospect. More tourists may create more jobs, but it also reduces the Balinese attachment to other sources of income which are of immense

14

traditional importance. A recent example was the sale of land by rice farmers near Tanah Lot to an international hotel group which built a luxury complex. The importance of tourism is logical and yet questionable, bearing in mind the economic dependence it creates.

Anniversary celebrations, and a new era

Politics and administration

President Suharto has been the head of state of the Republic of Indonesia since 1968. According to its constitution, Indonesia is a centrally governed presidential republic based on the national doctrine *pancasila*, the five (*panca*) principles which have been declared the pillars (*sila*) of the state. These principles are the belief in a single all-powerful God, together with humanity, national unity, democracy and social equality. The national motto, intended to hold together the multiplicity of peoples that make up the nation, is taken from a Javan epic: *Bhinneka Tunggal Ika* – Unity in Diversity.

Indonesia is not a democracy in the Western sense of the word. It was Suharto's predecessor, President Sukarno, who coined the phrase 'Guided Democracy'. Power is concentrated in the hands of the president, who rules in an authoritarian manner and who silences opponents and critics. Suharto's Western allies have protested against his treatment of separatist movements, such as the one in East Timor. As the protest movements have become more energetic, hopes of a gradual democratisation have grown.

Indonesia is divided into 27 provinces, of which Bali is one. The governor, who resides in Denpasar, is answerable to the Ministry of the Interior in Jakarta. The province of Bali is subdivided into eight regions (*kabupaten*), each with a capital: Badung (Denpasar), Bangli (Bangli), Buleleng (Singajara), Gianyar (Gianyar), Jembrana (Negara), Karangasem (Amlapura), Klungkung (Semarapura) and Tabanan (Tabanan).

Flying the flag

Historical Highlights

Middle of the third millennium BC The first wave of migrants arrives in Indonesia from present-day south China.

1500BC The first megalithic monuments are found in Indonesia.

500BC Bronze Age culture on Bali.

AD500 Buddhism infiltrates the island.

1000 Dharmawanga, an East Javanese king, assumes power over Bali. Erlangga, a Balinese prince, becomes king in east Java, influencing culture in Bali. The *Ramayana* and *Mahabharata* are translated into old Javanese (Kawi) script. Bali becomes independent.

1100 The 'Mother Temple' Besakih is built.

End of 13th century the Majapahit dynasty gains power on Java, ruling over an area corresponding with that of present-day Indonesia. The Pejeng dynasty rules on Bali.

15th century Islam reaches Java and precipitates the fall of the Majapahit dynasty. The elite flee to Bali, where the son of the last ruler has himself proclaimed raja (king) of Bali in Gelgel. He founds the Gelgel dynasty and assumes the title *Dewa Agung*. The seeds of what is today regarded as typical Balinese culture and religion are sown.

Early 16th century A unified Bali conquers territories in East Java and Lombok. The first Europeans arrive in Southeast Asia. Initially, Portugal and Spain's main interest lies in the spices on the Moluccas. During the second half of the century they are followed by the Dutch, who land on Bali for the first time in 1597. In 1602 the Dutch East India Company is founded to exploit Indonesia more effectively.

17th century Batavia is founded by the Dutch. The decline of the Dewa Agung allows a number of principalities to assert their independence and several autonomous Hindu kingdoms are created. Nonetheless, the Dewa Agung remains the highest-ranking raja on Bali. For religious reasons, the seat of government is moved to Klungkung.

17th–18th centuries The Raja of Karangasem becomes the most powerful ruler on Bali, and manages at times to gain control over Lombok. Bali is divided by continual feuds amongst the various princes.

1799 The Dutch East India Company goes bankrupt and the government of the Netherlands takes over the administration of the archipelago. Indonesia becomes a colony.

1846 The first Dutch military expedition lands in Baleng (North Bali). A few years later, the first Dutch regent establishes his headquarters in Singaraja. North Bali is henceforth ruled by the Dutch. New laws make slavery illegal and ban *suttee*, the self-immolation by widows in the cremation fires of their husbands.

1900 The Raja of Gianyar seeks colonial protection from the other principalities who continue their internecine feuds instead of forming an alliance against the colonial rulers.

1904 Dutch attempts to colonise the island by force from their base in Singaraja but meets with violent opposition by the South Bali rajas. The situation becomes acute when the trading ship *Sri Muala* runs aground near Sanur. Locals plunder the wreckage. The owners demand the return of the cargo or repayment. The Dutch passes the request on to Raja Agung Made of Badung. The raja says beachcombing is a Balinese tradition and refuses to offer any compensation.

1906 After two years of fruitless negotiations, the colonial government takes the incident as a welcome excuse to declare war. A violent Dutch attack ends in ritual suicide (*puputan*) in Badung. Colonial troops march to the prince's palace but the Balinese with hopelessly inferior weapons, are too proud to surrender. Dressed in white, 2,000 Balinese die, including women and children at the hands of the Dutch. Those not shot by Dutch rifles, draw their *kris* and kill their wounded friends, wives and children to spare them the shame of capture.

1908 A similar Balinese *puputan* against foreign rule takes place in Klungkung and the Battle of Marga (*see page 34*). The island falls into

Dutch hands. The rajas are deprived of their powers but remain important art patrons.

1920–40 A growing Indonesian nationalist movement is repressed by the Dutch. The colonial government decides to 'protect and preserve' Bali from outside influences and exploitation. An artistic and cultural revival is inspired by visiting foreign artists and writers, anthropologists and musicologists, such as Walter Spies, Rudolf Bonnet and Vicki Baum.

1937 Baum's novel *A Tale from Bali*, describes traditions and religious practices of everyday life in a Bali village against the background of the *puputan*. Another popular novel set against the background of the War of Independence is *K'tut Tantri – Revolt in Paradise*, tells of an American girl adopted by a prince of the Bangli dynasty.

1942 The Japanese invade Indonesia and remain until the end of World War II in 1945. To win local support, they give the principal nationalist leader, General Sukarno (1901–70), considerable political latitude.

---

17 August 1945 General Sukarno proclaims Indonesian independence to become its first president. The Dutch return. For four years there is extensive fighting between the occupying forces and guerrilla groups. Bali is pro-Dutch.

---

20 November 1946 In the Battle of Marga in Central Bali (*see page 34*), the country's national hero I Gusti Ngurah Rai and 94 patriots are killed fighting the Dutch.

1949 The Dutch confirm the independence of the Republic of Indonesia under President Sukarno, with Bali becoming a province. However, economic difficulties drive the new state into bankruptcy. Sukarno abandons his Western alliances and withdraws into political isolation.

1963 Gunung Agung erupts. Thousands of people are killed on Bali, and many temples and villages are destroyed.

1965 A coup attempt is made against President Sukarno. Official reports claim General Suharto, head of the army's strategic command, defeated a communist uprising and the government devotes its energies to persecuting

communism. Even Bali is not spared the bloody consequences and between 100,000 and 200,000 people are executed throughout the country. Suharto, his eyes on the leadership, persuades Sukarno to hand over effective power to him.

1968 General Suharto (born 1921) is elected President of Indonesia, and is subsequently re-elected for seven terms. His New Order helps the national economy prosper and direct investment and loans from the West are encouraged, but not Western-style democracy.

1970 The growth in mass tourism begins, eventually transforming Bali from a hippy haven into a resort island. The island is the subject of the first-ever *Insight Guide*.

1975 Indonesia occupies East Timor, a former Portuguese territory and continues to occupy it, despite continuing United Nations and human rights protests, with a large military force.

1979 The Eka Dasa Rudra ritual purification, which takes place once a century, is held at Besakih temple.

1986 Nusa Dua is developed into an upmarket tourist enclave.

1993 Plans to build a gigantic *garuda* bird statue and amusement park near the airport lead to serious protests.

1994 Uproar over resort development at Tanah Lot temple area. Hindus unite across Indonesia to protest about the proposal.

1997 Indonesia enters the Asian economic crisis. The rupiah is devalued and basic commodity prices soar. Suharto has to make a US$43 billion bail-out deal with the International Monetary Fund.

1998 President Suharto is re-elected for his sixth five-year term. Mobs demonstrate over food prices. Students protest over hike in petrol prices and political corruption, and it escalates into massive riots and looting in Jakarta. Bali remains peaceful. The student protests lead to Suharto's resignation May 21 and installation of vice-president, Dr Bacharuddin Jusuf Habibie, as Indonesia's third president.

Above: Sanur beach
Preceding pages:
Pura Ulun Danu on Lake Bratan

Route 1

The South

Kuta/Legian, Sanur and Nusa Dua

Bali's 'built-up tourist areas' are concentrated in the south of the island. The reasons for the development of the tourist infrastructure along this previously quiet coastal strip are clear: endless beaches, the proximity of Ngurah Rai airport and the capital city of Denpasar. With an average density of more than 1,000 inhabitants per sq km (2,770 per sq mile), this area is the most heavily populated region on the island, the people drawn by the tourist boom and better employment opportunities.

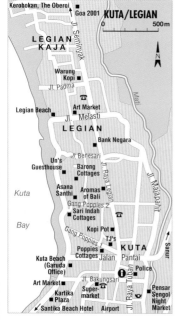

Kuta/Legian

These two fishing villages, which once lay several kilometres apart on the island's most beautiful beach, were the epitome of paradise for the hippies and world travellers who arrived on Bali during the 1960s. They have long since become the largest tourist development area on the island. No fewer than 300 dwellings, from simple *losmen* to international luxury hotels, shelter mostly younger tourists from the West, along with large numbers of Australians. The main tourist axis leads along Jalan Raya Legian, the central road linking the two centres. The traffic is heavy with an endless stream of cars and motorbikes, and along the sides, shops, restaurants, cafés, street traders, money changers, car and motorcycle rental companies are lined up in colourful profusion. Hordes of sun-worshippers, watersports fiends and surfers crowd Kuta, famous for its beach, surf and gorgeous sunsets. The street traders regard the beach to all intents and purposes as another shopping street, and a beach massage is also part of the entertainment on offer. At night, Jalan Raya Legian comes alive with a rash of fashionable nightspots and restaurants serving everything from Italian pastas to Indonesian *nasi padang*. Jalan Pantai Kuta, running along the beach, is no quieter but in some of the side streets linking the two roads it is still possible to find hints of Kuta's former village life. If your first instinct is to flee from the spectre of mass tourism in Kuta, and yet you want to be near it, settle for the much quieter and more relaxed Legian or stay further north at Seminyak.

Kuta beach

Sanur

Luminaries like novelist Vicki Baum, who used Sanur as the setting for her book, *A Tale from Bali*, and the Belgian painter Adnen Jean Le Mayeur de Mepres put the quiet fishing village on to the world travel map during the 1930s. In 1966, the opening of the Hotel Bali Beach, built as wartime reparation by the Japanese, marked the beginning of Sanur's rapid development from a malaria-infested swamp to a world-class resort. Relatively more sedate and expensive than Kuta, Sanur always has enjoyed a more up-market image, although is getting increasingly crowded with shops and restaurants. There is a wide selection of spacious hotel complexes in typical local bungalow style. As a result of the stronger tidal currents on the east coast, the water retreats as far as the offshore coral reef, making swimming almost impossible at low tide.

Young festival participant

21

Nusa Dua

The private enclave of Nusa Dua – which means 'two islands' – covers an area of several hundred hectares in the east of the Bukit Badung peninsula. This self-contained area was conceived during the early 1970s, when mass tourism began to take a hold on Bali, and was partly financed with funds from the World Bank. The government's main aim was to restrict tourist development to specific areas and keep the locals away from the inevitable results of mass tourism.

The project has certainly fulfilled the government's aims as far as separating tourists from the daily life of the local inhabitants is concerned. In 1983, the Nusa Dua Beach Hotel opened as the first of a series of a dozen luxury hotels in the area. It is difficult for a guest to believe that Bali is still part of the third world when comfortably ensconced

Nusa Dua beach and hotel pool

Bali Museum, exhibits

within the confines of a luxury hotel surrounded by immaculately landscaped gardens. Pampered holiday-makers who long for sun and sand and the occasional taste of the island's culture will feel at home here.

All Nusa Dua hotels are in the luxury category and have facilities like swimming pools, restaurants and shopping. 'Balinese Evenings' with a buffet and dance performance, package the island's culture for visitors.

Excursions
Denpasar

The capital of Bali province (pop. 370,000) also is the island's economic and administrative hub. The town was previously known as Badung, and was at one stage the royal capital of the kingdom of the same name. In 1945, the administrative centre of the province of Bali was moved from Singaraja to Badung. When Indonesia declared independence, the town was rechristened Denpasar and from this point the settlement rapidly grew into a town. Most tourists avoid the traffic chaos of the capital, but it is nonetheless worth at least a short visit. The market and museum, in any case, should not be missed.

The route to the sights of Denpasar leads to the **Puputan Square** in the centre of the town. A memorial similar to the one found in many Balinese villages commemorates the *puputan* massacre of 1906 (*see page 16*).

The ★**Bali Museum** (Tuesday to Thursday 8am–4pm, Friday 8am–1pm, Saturday 8am–2pm and Sunday 8am–2pm, closed Monday) lies to the east of the square. It provides an excellent introduction to Balinese art and culture from the early history of the island to the present day. Housed in a spacious complex created by the Dutch in 1932, the museum combines the architectural styles of palaces and temples in the north, east and west of Bali to create a colourful whole. The individual collections are divided between four buildings and contain masks, shadow puppets, ritual objects, pottery and woodcarvings as well as an attractive picture display describing the rites of passage (*see page 71–2*). Of note amongst the archaeological finds and prehistoric exhibits are the stone sarcophagi. The modern building complex contains examples of traditional and modern painting and Balinese crafts.

From the *kulkul* (alarm drum) tower on the left of the split gate marking the museum entrance, the perspective widens to reveal the **Pura Jagatnata** to the north. In the sanctuary of this royal temple the universal deity Sang Hyang Widhi Wasa is worshipped. The deity is the symbol of faith in the one almighty God in accordance with the Indonesian national doctrine. The massive Lotus Throne dominating the complex bears a metal relief depicting Sang Hyang Widhi Wasa dancing.

Behind the pura rises the tower of the Catholic **Church of St Joseph**. The church's entrance is on Jalan Kepundung. The decoration is a charming mixture of Christian pictorial details and Balinese elements. The reliefs decorating the facade are reminiscent of Balinese temples, and the angels dressed in sarongs bear a strong resemblance to Legong dancers.

Pura Jagatnata and the Church of St. Joseph

Jalan Gajah Mada and the side streets Jalan Kartini and Jalan Sulawesi bustle with life. They are full of textiles, antique and craft shops stocked with wares that are mostly cheaper than those in the tourist centres of the island.

A stroll across the ★**Pasar Badung** (market) allows you to immerse yourself in the everyday life of the island by observing Balinese housewives buying fresh produce. On the other side of the river lies **Pasar Kumbasari**, a shopping centre for crafts designed to appeal to mass taste. There also are restaurants here.

If you have developed a taste for Balinese art, you should visit the **Werdhi Budaya Art Centre** on Jalan Bayasuta on the eastern edge of town (daily 8am–4pm). The architecture of the individual pavilions is worth seeing in itself. Inside you will find works by Balinese painters and wood carvers, and exhibitions of items for sale are sometimes held. A separate section commemorates the work of the German artist Walter Spies. Every evening the complex comes to life when groups of tourists come to watch the excellent Kecak dance performances (*see page 78*), which begin at 6.30pm.

Werdhi Budaya Art Centre

Bukit Badung Peninsula

Bukit (*Bukit* meaning 'hill') **Badung**, at Bali's southernmost tip, is largely devoid of vegetation apart from scrub and cactus, standing in stark contrast to the tropical flora which abounds in the irrigated eastern section of the peninsula, the tourist centre of Nusa Dua. In the northwest of

Spectacular Pura Ulu Watu

Bukit Badung, to the south of the airport, lies **Jimbaran Beach**, a new resort area, previously ignored by the architects of tourism in Bali. Discovered only in the past few years, the beach has already attracted deluxe resort developments such as the Four Seasons Ritz-Carlton and the Inter-Continental group. For the moment at least, one can enjoy the quiet atmosphere and the clean waters of its white-sand beach.

From here, after following a winding road for about 25km (16 miles), you will reach ★★**Pura Ulu Watu**, thought to have been founded at the turn of the first millennium ad. Like Pura Tanah Lot (*see page 35*), this is one of the six holy 'national' sea temples on the island. The journey is worthwhile just to see its spectacular location on the cliffs overlooking the pounding surf.

The temple is dedicated to Dewi Danu, the ruler of the lakes who, according to Balinese legend, landed on the island here at Ulu Watu. The rocky plateau on which the temple stands is said to be her ship, which was transformed into stone. A hundred metres below, the waves dash themselves against the rocks. Up by the temple you sense the power of the elements and the threat they pose to people. In such surroundings the Balinese feel in need of protection, but foreign surf fans are happy to ride the dangerous waves off Suluban Beach.

Nusa Penida and Nusa Lembongan

These two sparsely populated and arid islands, off the southeast coast of Bali, have very little in common with the tropically lush main island. **Nusa Penida** covers an area of over 300sq km (114sq miles). Its arid highlands extend across a limestone plateau, giving the island its distinctive silhouette. Fishing, maize and vegetable farming are the main occupations for the 40,000 islanders, most of them Muslim. A visit to the fishing village of **Toya-pakeh** in the northeast of the island will provide a glimpse of their everyday life.

The Balinese regard the island as inhospitable and, according to legend, it is the home of demons and evil spirits. The fearful giant Jero Gede Mecaling, who brings misfortune and illness, is said to be an inhabitant. For prisoners formerly banished here by the Balinese rulers, there was no worse place of exile. Trips to the island, which is still largely undeveloped, can be arranged in Sanur.

Surfers and divers should try and spend a few days on the neighbouring island of **Nusa Lembongan**. The island's protective coral reef and massive waves attract mostly Australian surfers, who frequently stay in the numerous *losmen* in Jungutbatu. Catamarans and refitted traditional **pinisi** vessels sail daily to both islands from Benoa Harbour.

Route 2

Ubud and environs

The cultural heart of Bali is a region where picturesque countryside, artistry and life in a village community still rich in traditions are blended into a harmonious whole. Ubud and the surrounding villages in the central Balinese province of Gianyar have more or less grown together as a result of the tourist development during the past few decades. The town itself takes its name from *ubad*, Balinese for medicine, stemming from the healing properties of a herb growing near the Campuhan river.

Ubud market and puppet making

Now Ubud is the home of painters and dancers, and this is where increasing numbers of foreign artists have made their home since the 1920s. Ubud's fame as the centre of artistic skills on the island spread rapidly throughout the West, and the ensuing tourist development was therefore inevitable. Ubud is the very epitome of the scenic beauty and cultural richness which characterise Bali. The combination proves irresistible for many visitors. With a dozen temples in the area, there is a good chance to witness a few of the colourful religious temple ceremonies during your stay.

25

Bearing in mind the size of Ubud and its population of around 9,000, the vast range of accommodation and

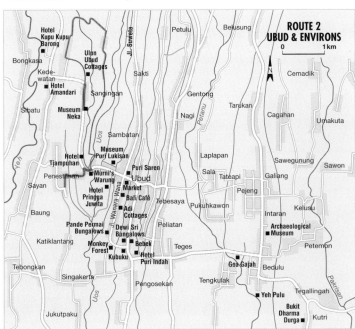

A variety of headgear

restaurants competing for the attention of tourists – not to mention the rampant commerce – may seem overwhelming. Visitors hoping to escape the area entirely can head for the surrounding villages – Campuhan, Peliatan or Pengosekan – which provide a better chance of experiencing life in a real Balinese village community. Having left the bustle of Jalan Ubud Raya, the main east-west artery, and Jalan Wanara Wana (the Monkey Forest Road) which forms the main thoroughfare running from north to south, you will find yourself in the heart of rural Bali, where you can delight in the honking of geese and the cool breeze wafting through the rice fields.

Ubud's favourable location makes it an ideal base for excursions. You can visit some of the oldest temples on the island or explore the delights of the local countryside by just walking. The region is criss-crossed by a network of narrow but mostly well constructed roads linking the many villages around Ubud with each other. With the aid of a route map, the area also is ideal for a bicycle tour (the best place to hire bicycles is Ubud itself).

Losmen are run by local families

One of the most congenial, and the most inexpensive, places to stay is at a *losmen* run by local families. Whether you settle for this option or one of the typical bungalow complexes set in a tranquil garden ablaze with tropical flowers, you will quickly feel at home.

Visitors to Ubud can see one of the daily dance performances which are generally regarded as being the best the island has to offer. Information concerning the various cultural and other events, temple festivals as well as tickets for the events themselves can be obtained from the **Bina Wisata Tourist Centre** on Jalan Ubud Raya. Even sports fans will find plenty to appeal to them, as there are excellent opportunities for river rafting in the **Sayan Valley** (*see page 85*).

Rafting in the Sayan Valley

Western painters came to Bali during the early years of the 20th century. They sought inspiration in the tropical landscape as well as the works of the local artists. Two of the first arrivals were Walter Spies, the German painter and musician, as well as a Dutch artist, Rudolf Bonnet. They settled in Campuhan, in those days a separate village which today is a district of Ubud, where they began a detailed study of Balinese painting. During the 1930s, together with nobleman Cokorda Gde Agung Sukawati, they founded an artists' association known as Pita Maha (see page 74). This initiative inspired an artistic renaissance, transforming sleepy Ubud village, into a centre of cultural revolution.

The tradition and importance of painting in Ubud can be seen not least in the three most important art museums here. Would-be art purchasers will find here a useful summary of the principal genres and types of art practised in Bali. Behind the Pura Saraswati temple in the heart of the town lies the ★★**Puri Lukisan Museum** ('Palace of Paintings', open daily 8am–4pm). Opened in 1956, the museum owes its existence to the efforts of Rudolf Bonnet. It contains an excellent collection of Balinese painting and traces the development of wood carving. Some of the displays here are for sale.

The Puri Lukisan Museum exhibits local works

27

Visitors can either walk or take a *bemo* from Central Ubud to the ★★**Neka Museum** (daily 9am–5pm), which lies some 2km (1 mile) north of Campuan, on the road to Kedewatan. It is named after Suteja Neka, a native of Ubud. The son of a renowned woodcarver, Neka was an avid art collector and a member of the Pita Maha group. His museum, which opened in 1982, aims to educate foreigners on the development of Balinese painting from the traditional *wayang* style to contemporary forms of artistic expression.

Neka Museum, entrance detail and exhibit

The museum's art collection is distributed between four pavilions. The first contains the development from the *wayang* style through the Ubud/Batuan style to representative works by the so-called Young Artists (*see page 28*). The second pavilion is devoted to outstanding Balinese artists, including Gusti Nyoman Lempad, who died in 1978 at the age of 116. Lempad's detailed ink drawings of barong heads, cremation towers and temple reliefs influenced an entire school of art. The next pavilion displays the works of Balinese and Javanese artists who retain a strong traditional accent in their work despite the obvious Western influence. The last pavilion houses works by exceptional Indonesian artists, in particular the eccentric Javanese Affandi (1907–90). On the upper floor are works by foreign artists who were influenced by Balinese art and who in turn influenced local painters. The

An immersion in rural Bali

collection includes paintings by Rudolf Bonnet, Arie Smit and the painters Han Snel and Antonio Maria Blanco, both of whom still live in Ubud. The only example of the works of Walter Spies is a copy of one of his paintings. Not a single original work of Spies has remained on the island; all his pictures are now in private collections elsewhere in the world.

★★**Agung Rai Museum of Art** (ARMA), in Pengosekan, Tel: 0361-976659, houses an impressive collection of traditional and modern Balinese paintings and works on Bali by foreign artists. The permanent collection should not be missed. Open 9am–6pm daily.

Visitors who now want to feast their senses on the wonders of the Balinese landscape should embark on the three-hour ★★**walk to Campuhan**. From the Neka Museum the path leads for about 400m (¼ mile) in a northerly direction as far as Sangingan, where it passes the Ulun Ubud Cottages before turning west. Walkers can immerse themselves in the reality of everyday life on Bali as depicted in museum paintings. Narrow footpaths lead between rice paddies, before continuing along the main street of the village. After following the asphalt road for a short way, the path turns around a long bend and crosses a bridge before coming to the most attractive section of all, above the River Uos.

After about 3km (2 miles), the route joins the main road from Ubud to Campuhan, not far from the bridge. Beside the bridge is Murni's Warung, where you can stop for refreshments, or head for the restaurant at the nearby Hotel Tjampuhan. Walter Spies lived here at the end of the 1930s, until the stream of visitors became too much for him and he retired to Iseh in the Karangasem area.

The walk can be continued from Campuhan. From the bridge there is a narrow path leading uphill away from the main road. The track leads between the rice paddies to **Penestanan**, which is about 30 minutes away. During the 1960s, the village was a gathering place for local schoolchildren and young people who studied with the Dutch painter Arie Smit. The group came to be known as the 'Young Artists', and produced its own characteristic style of painting.

Ubud market
Puri Saren, detail

Back in the centre of Ubud, the **market** provides a chance to marvel at the array of tropical fruits. The market is also particularly good for inexpensive trinkets and crafts. Be sure to get there early, though – it's dead by 2pm.

To the north of the market lies **Puri Saren**, the residence of the princely Sukawati family. The palace, with its gateways and courtyards, is still partly inhabited today, although one wing has been turned into a hotel.

Monkey Forest Road, Jalan Wanara Wana, leads away from the centre in a southerly direction. About 2km (1 mile) long, it is bordered on both sides by restaurants, shops and hotels. At the beginning of the 1980s it was just a quiet village street, but now it demonstrates all too clearly the extent to which tourism is developing on the island has utterly transformed the surroundings. It's best to do this walk in the early morning or late afternoon because the midday sun can be merciless.

Puri Saren: palatial trimmings

29

The monkeys can be aggressive

At ★**Monkey Forest**, visitors come face to face with a band of half-tame grey monkeys. Vendors sell bananas and peanuts outside the forest entrance but resist the temptation to feed them. They tend to be aggressive and have been known to bite people. Conceal from view any items that can be easily snatched by the monkeys – like spectacles, earrings and handbags. The local inhabitants revere the monkeys, whom they regard as the sacred descendants of legendary monkey general Hanuman.

Descending the steps from the entrance into the forest, it is hard not to be enchanted by the vast *waringin* tree, regarded as sacred by the Balinese. At the other side of the bridge is the **Pura Beji**, a small temple tucked away in the forest, and a sacred spring.

Pura Dalem Agung Padang Tegal

Continuing to the right of the waringin tree, is the temple of the underworld, ★**Pura Dalem Agung Padang Tegal**. Its covered gateway, which leads to the inner temple courtyard, stands on the back of the giant tortoise Bedawang. Entwined by two snakes, the gateway symbolises the underworld. Temples of death are dedicated to Durga, the goddess of death, who also can assume the form of the witch Rangda. Indicative of this fact are the stone Rangda sculptures, whose huge hanging breasts touch the ground and are said to guarantee fertility, whilst the tongues of fire also lick at the earth and make it vulnerable to destruction.

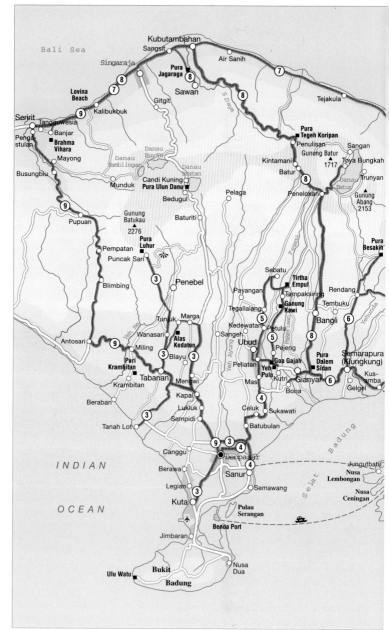

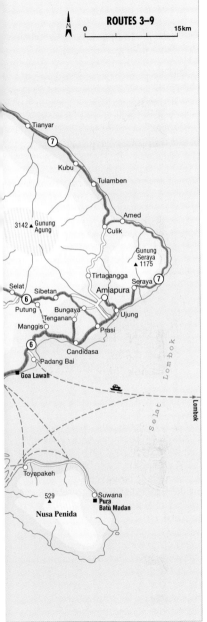

ROUTES 3–9

0   15km

Tianyar

Kubu

Tulamben

Amed

3142 ▲ Gunung Agung

Culik

Gunung Seraya ▲ 1175

Tirtagangga

Seraya

Selat

Sibetan

Amlapura

Putung

Bungaya

Ujung

Tenganan

Manggis

Prasi

Candidasa

Padang Bai

Goa Lawah

Selat Lombok

Lombok

Toyapakeh

529 ▲

Suwana

Pura Batu Madan

Nusa Penida

Rice paddies, Route 3

North coast, Route 7

Temple of the Dead, Route 8

Route 3

Temples of mountain and sea

Mengwi – Alas Kedaton – Marga – Gunung Batukau – Pura Luhur – Tanah Lot *See map on pages 30–1*

The journey to the holy places of mountain and sea leads from the sea (*kelod*), the realm of the demons, towards the mountains of the island's interior (*kaja*), the home of the gods. On the way you pass three very different temples. Taman Ayun in Mengwi is one of the loveliest on Bali. With Pura Luhur, it is the mysterious location at the foot of the volcano Gunung Batukau which is the main attraction. At the final temple, Tanah Lot, the dramatic setting of jagged-edged cliffs amidst crashing waves and the temple itself silhouetted against the setting sun, enthrall. The drive leads through an alternating landscape of mountains with rice terraces. This is a full-day excursion, so set out early and return before nightfall.

Ruling the road

Visitors approaching from the south can take a short cut through Canggu, visiting Tanah Lot first. Those coming from Sanur should follow the ring road to the north and east of the town before setting out in the direction of Mengwi and Tanah Lot. Even here on the outskirts, Denpasar's roads seem hopelessly inadequate for today's traffic. Eventually, however, the metropolis is left behind and new perspectives open up.

Fresh produce at Pura Taman Ayun

In the more densely populated parts of the island some stretches of road lead through an endless succession of villages which seem to form a single mass area. The passing tourist will be overwhelmed by a wealth of interesting scenes. In villages bordering the route are countless examples of the artistic creativity of the Balinese. In **Kapal**, for instance, the road runs through an apparent sculpture garden surrounded by the workshops of potters, stonemasons and cement workers. For generations, these village craftsmen have created elaborate decorative fixtures for Balinese temples and house fronts throughout the island.

Creativity is a Balinese hallmark

A few kilometres further (17km/11 miles from Denpasar) a turn right leads to ★★★**Pura Taman Ayun**. This is the second most important temple in Bali (after Pura Besakih, *see page 45*). Visitors wishing to experience its peaceful ceremonial atmosphere should aim to arrive as early as possible, before the hordes of tourists descend. In the early hours of the morning, it seems as if nothing could interrupt the tranquillity of the custodian bending over his short-handled broom, sweeping up the leaves and blossoms from the frangipani tree.

As you enter the first courtyard, your gaze is drawn towards the *kulkul* bell tower to the left of the main gateway. A narrow staircase leads up to a broad platform providing the best view of the complex which is clearly divided into three terraced courtyards. The Pura Taman Ayun is a perfect example of the harmonious principles underlying Balinese temple architecture. Surrounded by moats covered with lotus blossoms, the 'Garden Temple on the Water' stands on an artificial island.

The term *taman* is reserved for temples which are at least partly surrounded by water. The Pura Taman Ayun is dedicated to the *Widadari*, the 'heavenly nymphs' sent from heaven to bathe at this spot. In the complex's southwestern corner is a square basin surrounded by demon statues. They mark the points of the compass and indicate the boundaries of the underworld. To the north, a series of terraces ascends the mountainside towards the gods' home.

The *jeroan* is the highest and most sacred courtyard. It is not open to visitors, but contains 29 shrines, some elaborately decorated with up to 11 meru roofs (*see page 70*). These symbolise the trees of heaven as they soar skywards into the realm of the gods, inviting them to descend to earth. Here, too, stands the triple lotus throne, the *padmasana*, the seat of honour reserved for the *trimurti*, trinity of the three principal deities Shiva, Vishnu and Brahma. Several smaller, more modest shrines are dedicated to various mountain deities.

33

The Pura Taman Ayun is one of the so-called royal temples and is held in awe by all Balinese. Its importance goes back to I Gusti Agung Anom, a member of a minor branch of the Gelgel dynasty, who founded the once-powerful Mengwi kingdom.

Pura Taman Ayun

Leave the temple and return through Mengwi to the original turn off junction. Turning right here, the route continues along the main road towards Bedugul (Lake Bratan) and Singaraja. After about 3km (2 miles), turn left/west direction (look out for the sign to Marga) along a minor road which leads to Peken. Just ahead is **Alas Kedaton Monkey Forest**. The Balinese believe that the hundreds of grey monkeys living in the trees here are macaque descendants of the brave troops of the legendary monkey general Hanuman. Unlike the monkeys in the forest of Sangeh, who are often disturbed by visitors and are therefore much more aggressive, those at Alas Kedaton are less visited and worshipped by the islanders. A walk through the forest provides good opportunities to observe their habits.

Marga's puputan memorial

Turning your back on the monkeys in the forest and the trader stalls around the entrance, continue along the road to ★**Marga**. Here, Balinese history comes alive on the drive along the wide approach road to the memorial. Surrounded by a broad lawn, the monument to the island's heroes radiates an aura of melancholy peace. The inscriptions recall the events of 20 November 1946, which turned Marga into the setting for a puputan (*see pages 16–17*), in this instance the ritual suicide of a band of Balinese resistance fighters under their general I Gusti Ngurah Rai. A Buddhist reliquary was erected on the adjoining cemetery to honour the fallen soldiers. The exhibits and photographs in the little museum tell the moving tale of the Balinese and Indonesian struggle for independence more graphically than anywhere else on the island.

From Marga, the poorly maintained narrow road, continues westwards as far as Tunjuk. Here, it turns south and, after passing through Beng and Calagi, eventually joins the surfaced main road north to **Gunung Batukau**. Take care not to miss the turn in Sekartaji. Continuing up towards the summit of the second-highest mountain on Bali (2,276m/7,467ft), the road leads the way to the home of the gods across the peaks of the central mountain chain.

By early afternoon, the mountain peaks often retreat from view behind a thick curtain of clouds. The rice-terrace landscape, formed over the centuries by human hands from the fertile volcanic soil, resembles a single vast sculpture. Supported by clay walls, the narrow terraces of rice paddies curve gently as they follow the contours of the hillside. In some places they rise up the slopes gradually, whilst in others they climb steeply towards the summit. Where the fields are flooded but not yet planted, the clouds and palm fronds are reflected in the water's surface. In other fields, the young rice seedlings gleam emerald green

The paddies follow the contours

in the sunlight as far as the eye can see. The horizon shimmers in a haze of blue, out of which rise the contours of the mountain chain. For many visitors, this is a perfect photo opportunity.

Pura Luhur Batukau – evoking the mountain spirit

The journey continues uphill along a gently curving road for another 20km (13 miles) as far as ★**Pura Luhur Batukau**, the 'Coconut Shell Mountain'. The temple lies on the southeastern flank of the volcano. The last section of road from Wongaya Gede to the temple itself, 3km (2 miles) above the village, was widened in 1993 to improve access to the mountain temple, which was restored during the same year. The spacious complex extends across several levels on the hillside. It is an awe-inspiring location in a clearing surrounded by jungle. In the mossy stupa-like shrines you can sense the presence of Maha Dewi, the 'Spirit of the Mountain', who is worshipped here on festival days.

An artificial pond on the right-hand side is reminiscent of Pura Taman Ayun in Mengwi (*see page 32*). Like Taman Ayun, Pura Luhur is a 'national' temple. On special feast days, such as Galungan, which celebrates the victory of good over evil, crowds of brightly clothed pilgrims gather here to pray.

35

Visitors should start their return journey no later than 4pm. The first stage of the route heads south, reaching **Tabanan**, the capital of the administrative district of the same name, after 27km (17 miles). Continue a short distance along the main road towards Denpasar to arrive at the Tanah Lot turning, which lies just north of Kediri. Tabanan is the rice bowl of Bali, and in this typical countryside travellers witness rural lifestyle.

Glimpse the rural lifestyle

When the light is right, a Balinese sunset is a dramatic natural phenomenon. Legend has it that the ★★★**Pura Tanah Lot** sea temple was founded by the Hindu priest Nirartha. Perched on a rocky crag above the sea, this little temple is another of the island's six holy 'national' sites. Tanah Lot also is one of a series of protective shrines along the south coast dedicated to the deities and spirits of the sea. Believers from all over Bali bring offerings to the temple to placate demons which inhabit the sea, constantly threatening the human world. Locals also claim that Tanah Lot is a place of worship dedicated to Dewi Sri, the goddess of the rice harvest.

Pura Tanah Lot

As the sun sets, the tourist 'pilgrims' gather around the seats in front of the numerous cafés and drinks stands. The ever-changing light adds to the breathtakingly beautiful view and demands the patience of any photographer. Well-heeled visitors have a short walk to the Bali Nirwana luxury resort, one of the latest developments in the vicinity of the temple.

Barong dance in progress

Route 4

The Craftsmen's Road

Batubulan – Celuk – Mas – Peliatan – Ubud *See map on pages 30–1*

A stroll through the workshops and galleries fringing the road from Batubulan to Peliatan will emphasise the importance of art in the everyday life of the Balinese, whether you attend a *Barong* performance or a stonemason's studio in Batubulan, a silversmith's workshop in Celuk or admire the skills of the woodcarvers of Mas. If you want a change of scenery from the south, move up to Ubud (*see page 25*). Together with the surrounding villages, it remains the centre of Balinese painting. There is about one hour of driving on this route.

Batubulan lies only a few kilometres from the tourist centres of the south coast. Countless stone sculptures lined along the roadside leave no doubt that this is the centre of Balinese stonemasonry. Hindu gods and heroes stand beside Buddha heads, gnomes and other mythical creatures. The larger examples of these elaborately carved sandstone or Andesite lavastone figures are seen in hotels and restaurants throughout the island. However, the galleries and workshops also contain many works of art small enough to fit into a suitcase.

Temple decoration was the stonemason's preserve, but today frequent recourse is made to more permanent and cheaper cement castings. It is no coincidence, however, that Batubulan is the home of a temple, the ★**Pura Puseh Batubulan**, adorned with one of the finest examples of

Pura Puseh Batubulan

the stonemason's art. The two Buddha statues in niches on either side of the entrance are no doubt derived from Borobudur temple in Java. In any case, they indicate that the founder of Buddhist teaching is entitled to a place in the Balinese pantheon of gods.

Batubulan's other major attraction is the ★★★**Barong Dance** (*see page 78*). The stage is the oldest of four in the village. For more than 20 years, Barong and Rangda have fought here every morning between 9.30 and 10.30am. The exorcist ritual has become a tourist show, but it is so perfectly and charmingly executed that it is a must for every visitor. Those wishing to see the temple in peace, however, should arrive before 9am or after 11am.

The local gamelan band

The antique shops along the main road look tempting. But beware that many of the so-called genuine antique items for sale are no more than a few months old.

Jewellery fans should not miss out ★**Celuk**, only 2 km (3 miles) further north. The village is home to the island's gold- and silversmiths. The biggest galleries are on the main street, but bargain hunting is more fun in the little family-run businesses in the side streets, where you can watch craftsmen producing their delicate wares.

37

Sukawati is home to the most famous puppeteers (*dalangs*) on Bali. Their remarkable skills (*see page 77*) have not yet been exploited commercially. The village also boasts a colourful fruit and vegetable market. Near Sakah, leave the main road where it bends to the right/east. Continue straight ahead for a few kilometres to arrive in **Mas**. More Brahman families live here than anywhere else on the island. They can trace their origins back to the Javanese priest Nirartha, who established the caste system on Bali in the 16th century. Nowadays, Mas is better known as the woodcarvers' village. Unfortunately, commerce has won the battle against art for its own sake, and the range of galleries is bewildering. The exhibits are expensive and adapted to suit Western tastes. Nonetheless, the craftsmanship is excellent and the local artisans guarantee that they use ebony, in contrast to the cheap imitations in the markets, which are made of *sawo* wood dyed with shoe polish. The latter is likely to develop cracks as soon as it is transported to temperate climes.

Woodcarvers in Mas

Peliatan already is a suburb of Ubud. Its proximity can be deduced from the numerous art galleries and craftsmen's shops. Peliatan, however, is more famous as the home of dance groups which always win the annual Legong competition (*see pages 78–9*). The Bina Wisata Tourist Office in Ubud offers coach trips to its two theatres. Further on, a left turn leads back to Ubud. Along this road is Agung Rai Museum of Art (ARMA) (*see page 28*).

Route 5

Bali's oldest shrines

Ubud – Tegallalang – Tampaksiring – Gunung Kawi – Pejeng – Yeh Pulu – Goa Gajah *See map on pages 30–1, and also the map of Ubud on page 25*

Travel through spectacular Tegallalang valley with its startling views of lush rice terraces before visiting some of Bali's oldest temples and the world's largest bronze kettle drum cast in a single piece at Pejeng. Lovers of antiquities will enjoy the archaeological museum at Bedulu, the mysterious rock reliefs of Yeh Pulu and the meditation cave of Goa Gajah. This tour will easily take several hours and requires an early-morning start.

Leave Ubud in a northerly direction on the minor road to **Petulu**. At this hour the little village has no special attractions to offer. Plan to return one day at about 5pm, when hundreds of *kokokan* (white herons) return to roost in the trees after spending the day searching the surrounding rice fields for food. However, plan to watch from a safe distance if you do not fancy being rained upon by bird droppings.

Farmer in Tegalalang

The next stage of the journey is very picturesque. After a few kilometres, near the village of **Tegallalang**, the route passes through artistically designed ★**rice terraces** clinging to slopes above a river valley. Travelling traders discovered that this is a popular place with tourists. They lie in wait for visitors who stop to survey the scene. Most of the items on sale are brightly coloured wood carvings that Tegallalang village specialises in.

A short distance further on is **Pura Gunung Kawi**, a compact complex of 10 temples with spring and ritual bathing facilities. The moss-covered walls and statues look much older than they really are. Still, the complex affords a pleasant respite off the beaten tourist track.

A few kilometres to the east, near Tampaksiring, lies a more famous spring sanctuary, the ★**Pura Tirta Empul**, which lies on the upper reaches of the Pakerisan River. The spring in the centre of the temple is said to have been struck by the god Indra himself, thereby granting the heavenly hordes immortality.

Pura Tirtha Empul

Even today, the waters which feed the ritual bathing area at the front of the complex are said to possess remarkable powers. For many centuries, on a particular day of the year, a stone bearing Old Balinese inscriptions found in a nearby village was ritually washed together with masks and other cult objects, to renew their magic powers. Only recently, did scholars manage to decipher the text, which refers to the temple foundation in 962ad. The central pools have not been used as public bathing places since late 1960s. The best view of the bathing pools and the adjoining temple once was the prerogative of President Sukarno, who ruled Indonesia from 1945 to 1968 and had a summer palace built above the complex.

Temple detail

Return to the main road in the direction of Pejeng, retracing the route south. Along the way are some very interesting archaeological sites which bear witness to the wealth of the first recorded Balinese dynasty, which had its capital in Pejeng in the 10th and 11th centuries.

★★**Gunung Kawi** provides another highlight of the trip, both scenically and artistically. However, you first must descend 300 steep steps to enjoy the view of a lovely green valley flanked by precipitous rock walls. The descent is rewarded by nine huge rock *candi*. Four lie on one side of the river, five are on the opposite bank, reached by a bridge. These *candis* often are described as royal tombs, although no traces of human remains were ever found to support the view that this is a burial ground.

The term *candi* is Javanese, derived from a name of the Hindu goddess Durga, who was associated with a cult of the dead. Unlike in Bali, where the ashes of the deceased are scattered in the sea, Javanese *candi* are mostly mausoleums to hold the dead. In contrast to the Javanese variety, however, the Gunung Kawi *candis*, which are nothing more than carved reliefs without inner chambers, may have simply served as monuments in honour of Balinese kings.

They have massive stepped roofs and stand 7m (22ft) high in rock niches carved in the cliffs. Inscriptions, in a script used only between the late 10th and 11th centuries,

39

The candi of Gunung Kawi

Preparing offerings at Gunung Kawi

enabled accurate dating of the monuments. Deciphering the text, is difficult because the stones are weathered and language cryptic.

Scholars still cannot agree on which king is commemorated here. Some claim that the monuments were erected in honour of King Udayana and his family, especially his consort Mahendradatta. The latter was a princess from east Java who was largely responsible for bringing Javanese customs to the Balinese royal court. It was also due to Mahendradatta's influence that Old Javanese was adopted as the language of the court. The magic rites, which play an important part in Balinese religion and were derived from Indian Tantrism, probably came to the island with the Javanese.

Other experts regard the nine *candi* as a monument for Anak Wungsu, the brother of the famous Airlangga, and his eight wives or concubines. What is clear, though, is that the monument remains one of the most tangible examples of Javanese influence on Bali's culture. From the modest-looking temple beside the group of five *candi*, visitors enter a labyrinth-like sanctuary which was once probably a monastery. Together with a number of hermits' cells hewn into the rock, it hints at the important role which monks must have played in those days.

Big Balinese smiles

Ascending the steps, visitors can stop off at the nearby Restaurant Tampaksiring for a midday break before returning to the main road.

Pejeng is the next stop along this route. More than 40 temples containing well-preserved archaeological remains bear witness to the fact that Warmadeva, the first recorded Balinese king, founded a dynasty from which King Udayana also descended.

One attraction is the so-called ★'**Moon of Pejeng**' in

the **Pura Penataran Sasih**, thought to be the largest existing prehistoric bronze kettle drum in the world. It hangs in the northwest corner high in the temple. Cast in a single piece, it is both feared and revered by the Balinese. Shaped like an hourglass, it is beautifully etched and over 3m (10ft) long.

The Moon of Pejeng

There are a number of theories concerning its origin. The most plausible traces the kettle drum back to the Dongsong culture, Indonesia's first high civilisation, which spread across the whole of southeast Asia, and originating from Vietnam.

Less believable is the legend which relates that there were once 13 moons in the universe. One night, one of them fell from heaven and was caught in the branches of a tree. To the annoyance of a band of thieves, it turned night into day, making their work impossible. To extinguish light, one of the thieves clambered up the tree and urinated on the moon drum. The moon, however, exploded and fell to the ground, killing the villain instantly.

No one knows why this ancient kettle drum was placed so high. Anyone who wants to inspect it closely needs a telescope to make out the exquisite decorations on its stylised surface. Whatever the truth concerning its origins, this masterpiece certainly was made in Indonesia and dates from the 3rd century BC.

Pura Penataran Sasih, gardens and lingam-yoni forms

Many of the other temple shrines in Pejeng are decorated with stone objects hundreds of years old. These include figures of deities and representations of *lingam-yoni* forms - *lingam* representing the male and *yoni* the female principle.

The small archaeological museum of **Bedulu**, to the south of Pejeng on the way to the reliefs at Yeh Pulu, contains a number of fine sarcophagi, some in the shape of animals, dating from the 2nd and 3rd centuries BC. The village name is of interest, too, as it is derived from Bedahulu, which means 'exchanged head' and recalls the story of Raja Ratna Banten of the Pejeng dynasty.

The ruler was reputed to possess magic powers and as proof of his ability, he periodically allowed someone to decapitate him. On one occasion his powers failed and his despairing servant placed a pig's head on his shoulders. From then on, no one was permitted to see the Raja's head. By means of a trick, Gajah Mada, the prime minister of the Majapahit Kingdom of Java, was able to catch a glimpse of the deformed king. The king was literally consumed by flaming rage because of this impudent act.

The death during the mid-14th century of Raja Ratna Banten, whose palace stood on the site of the present village, paved the way for the invading armies of Java.

Yeh Pulu, reliefs and priestess

Nymphs at Goa Gajah

Outside Bedulu village is an interesting 10-minute walk across the rice fields to the enigmatic reliefs of ★★**Yeh Pulu**. In 1925, a relief frieze was excavated, 27m (88ft) long and 2m (7ft) high. Dating the find has prove extraordinarily difficult as nothing comparable ever has been found on Bali or Java. Most experts consider the Yeh Pulu reliefs to date from the 14th century, just before the Javanese invasion. The reliefs show scenes from daily life: a man carrying palm wine, bejewelled women, a priest, playful animals and a bear hunt. The latter gave rise to speculation that the carvings may depict scenes from the *Krishnayana*, the story of Krishna, an incarnation of the Hindu god Vishnu. The only god which is clearly identified is the elephant-headed Ganesha, the god of wisdom.

While Yeh Pulu is a tranquil spot, ★★★**Goa Gajah**, the 'Elephant Cave' on the main road is by contrast, much busier. The stone monster adorning the entrance to the cave was excavated in the 1920s. While it hardly is likely to arouse much fear, despite its bulging, squinting eyes and unkempt mane, the cave's gaping mouth is fantastically carved with the shapes of leaves, rocks, animals, waves and demons.

Exactly who or what is immortalised here in stone remains a mystery. The Balinese believe this carving, like the reliefs of Yeh Pulu and the *candi* of Gunung Kawi, is the work of the giant Kebo Iwo. They maintain that this monstrous stone creature is a self-portrait which the ogre scratched out of the rock with his fingernails during a single night. Or it might be a portrait of the giant Pasupati, who split Mount Mahameru – the Hindu holy mountain – into two parts and moved them to Bali in the form of the twin holy mountains of Gunung Agung and Gunung Batur.

By walking through the monster's mouth, visitors enter the throat of a T-shaped cave which once may have been a hermitage for Shivaist monks. The cave is airless and dark. It contains a triple lingam symbolising Shiva. There also is a Ganesha image which probably gave the cave its name. The open-air bathing quarters in front of the cave with its heavenly nymphs spouting water were discovered in the 1950s.

Remains of a Buddhist monastery, which is reached by staircase, indicate that Hindu and Buddhist monks probably lived here peacefully side by side. Of the two original Buddha statues once displayed here, only one remains, its head now missing. The second statue mysteriously disappeared years ago. The are both believed to date from about the 8th or 9th century.

From Goa Gajah it is a few minutes' drive back to Ubud. Returning to Sanur or Kuta will take about an hour.

Route 6

To the former capital and to the Mother Temple

Gianyar – Klungkung – Pura Besakih – Rendang – Putung – Candidasa *See map on pages 30–1*

Ikat at Gianyar

On this journey to the former royal capital and to the 'Mother Temple', you'll encounter terrifying paintings in the courtrooms of Klungkung and the most sacred temples on the island. East Bali also provides beautiful landscapes. You can walk across broad terraced rice fields and the thinly populated northeast coast lures visitors with unspoilt sandy beaches. The journey from Pura Besakih, the temple of heaven, to Amlapura crosses some of the loveliest scenery on the island. At Tirtagangga (*tirtha* means 'holy water'), weary travellers can take a refreshing swim in the spring-fed pool at the magnificent former water palace.

Visitors wishing to return to South Bali on the same day should take the route via Amlapura, Candidasa and continue along the southeast coast, stopping at Goa Lawah bat cave and in Kusamba, where the residents pan for salt. Those with enough time to spend a few days in the east should try and stay by the beach in Candidasa. Otherwise, head for the peace and scenic beauty of the village of Tirtagangga, but be ready to forgo creature comforts.

If starting from Ubud or the south, first drive eastwards through **Bona**, where there are numerous rattan furniture factories, and then through the textile centre of **Gianyar**. After 25km (16 miles), you arrive in **Klungkung** (**Semarapura**), which recently reverted to its original name. Klungkung is a bustling provincial capital which has played an important role in Bali's history. When the

Rattan produces fine furniture

refugees belonging to the Javanese Majapahit dynasty arrived on the island during the 11th century, they made their new home in the little village of Gelgel, 3km (2 miles) south of present-day Klungkung. The Majapahit ruler's son declared himself King of Bali and founded the Gelgel dynasty. During the 6th century, when Gelgel lost its supremacy as ruler of the island, Bali disintegrated into a series of independent principalities, many of which spent most of their time at war with the others.

In 1710, the seat of government was moved to Klungkung. The Raja of Gelgel remained the highest-ranking amongst the island princes and new his palace became the cultural centre of the island. The prince had his own personal troupe of dancers and musicians, gold- and silversmiths, as well as weapon forgers skilled in the art of making the traditional keris (*see page 75*). His artists, who were centred on nearby Kamasen, founded the wayang style of painting, which is sometimes known as the Kamasan school (*see page 74*).

The sovereignty of the rajas of Klungkung ended when the Dutch arrived on a punitive expedition, as they had done two years earlier in Badung. The Raja, his family and many faithful followers committed *puputan* or ritual suicide and the Dutch were rid of an unruly rebel. The royal palace, **Puri Semarapura**, was almost completely destroyed. Under Dutch colonial rule, however, two *bales* (pavilions) were expertly restored. As historic monuments offer an insight into the traditional Balinese style of painting, and provide a good impression of the complex's former magnificence.

Puri Semarapura

In the eastern corner of the palace, on Jalan Untung Surapati, stands ★★**Kerta Gosa**, the Court Hall. It once housed the island's supreme court. The customary law of the land (*adat*), which was handed down by word of mouth, varied from island to island and sometimes even from village to village.

Today, conflicts are normally dealt with in the first instance by the village community, and the opposing parties only go to court if an agreement cannot be reached. Bali's Supreme Court, presided over by three Brahmans, was situated in Klungkung until the Dutch arrival. The punishments ordained for the guilty party were draconian, as can be seen from the paintings on the ceiling. They depict women passing through fire as they gaze upon the faces of their aborted foetuses; adulterers whose genitals are burned away or thieves suffering an agonising death in cauldrons of boiling oil. The uppermost rows, by contrast, portray the joys of heaven. This pictorial representation of the Balinese view of the world shows heaven and hell as two essential components of the universe, the one unable to exist without the other.

View from Bukit Jambal

The adjoining **Bale Kembang** or Floating Pavilion, in the middle of the lotus pond, has ceilings which also are decorated with paintings. The building served as a reception or assembly hall.

Bale Kembang

To continue the journey to Pura Besakih, head north from Klungkung, passing the *puputan* monument. The road climbs gently at first, and with luck the sky may be cloudless for a clear view of Gunung Agung. Framed by rice fields, the sacred volcano's silhouette is magically powerful. Here and there the paddy fields are interspersed with fields of maize, soy beans, peanuts or chillies. The **Bukit Jambal** observation point road is bordered by clove trees and coffee plantations. The gradient soon becomes steeper and the bends sharper and Gunung Agung may occasionally disappear into the clouds. Evidence of the volcano's last eruption is still clearly visible in the streams of lava which left black traces along the river beds.

There is a large car park beneath the temple complex. Early in the morning it appears abandoned, but by noon it will be filled with coaches and lorries. The last kilometre of the journey must be completed on foot, and the countless souvenir shops lining the route make it difficult to assume the correct devotional posture. By the time pilgrims reach the main temple complex of ★★★**Pura Besakih**, many will be out of breath and perspiring.

Souvenirs at Pura Besakih
Pilgrims at the temple

The 'Mother Temple' is not a single edifice but rather a vast area containing more than 30 temple complexes housing over 200 different buildings. The individual shrines still bear, in some cases, their Old Balinese names, and not even the Hindu priests are in agreement as to their true significance. Pura Besakih is to the Balinese Hindu what St Peter's in Rome is to the practising Roman

Pura Besakih...

...the centre of Balinese Hinduism

Catholic. Its location is unique, for it lies at an altitude of 900m (3,000ft) on the slopes of the sacred volcano Gunung Agung. The Balinese always have regarded their mountains as holy, but no one quite knows when the first temple was erected on the abode of the gods. It is certain, however, that it must have been long before the arrival of the first Hindus on the island. There is evidence that a temple stood on this site as early as the 8th century and animist Hindu rituals took place here.

From the end of the 15th century the temple served as an ancestral shrine for the most powerful Balinese dynasty of the time, the Gelgel-Klungkung kings. Their descendants are still responsible for the upkeep of the Shiva complex. Higher-caste families own special shrines in Besakih, as do village communities and various professional groups.

One of the three most important temple complexes is **Pura Panataran Agung**, which is dedicated to Sang Hyang Widhi Wasa in his incarnation as Shiva. This does not prevent the Balinese from worshipping the trinity of Shiva, Brahma and Vishnu in the main courtyard. This one temple consists of some 60 individual edifices spread across seven ascending terraces.

To the east lies the second of the three main complexes, **Pura Kiduling Kreteng**, dedicated to Brahma and maintained by the Bangli royal family. Finally, to the west, lies the third 'trinity' temples, **Pura Batu Madeg**, dedicated to Vishnu. A staircase flanked by figures from the Mahabharata leads to the split gate, through which pilgrims can enter the Pura Panataran Agung temple courtyard. Only Hindus are allowed in. For other visitors there is a staircase which circumvents the temple and gives a good view of the main courtyard. The latter contains the shrines of the trinity, frequently covered with brightly coloured cloths. In the north-east corner of the temple complex is a little stall offering snacks and providing the best vantage point to view the landscape and beauty of this sacred and dignified place.

Pura Besakih is the setting for a highly important ritual. Once every century, the Eka Dasa Rudra, the greatest of Balinese sacrifices, is performed to purify the entire universe. During the years of colonial rule (after the 16th century), the sacrifice was not observed.

In the festive mood

At the beginning of the 1960s, however, the gods suddenly appeared to show their displeasure by sending a series of poor harvests and political unrest upon the island. The local priests were consulted and it seemed that the only way to put a stop to the island's misfortunes was to placate the gods with sacrificial offerings.

In February 1963, preparations for the Eka Dasa Rudra began. Suddenly, a glow of fire shone from the crater and Gunung Agung – which had not erupted for more than a century and was considered extinct – began to rumble. A priestess interpreted the ashes of the volcano as a sacred portent, and the people continued with their festival arrangements.

47

But soon after the sacrifice on 8 March, Gunung Agung erupted with unimaginable force. Large parts of eastern Bali were destroyed by the streams of lava, and more than 2,000 people were killed. As if by a miracle, however, the streams of lava split in two before they reached Pura Besakih and flowed past the sanctuary without damaging it. To most Balinese the eruption did not occur by chance, but was chastisement for having offended the gods. According to the Balinese *Saka* calendar, the islanders were not in fact supposed to celebrate the Eka Dasa Rudra until March 1979.

When that auspicious day finally came, the sacrifice was held without incident: the gods accepted the offerings and more than a million Balinese went to Gunung Agung to pay their respects to the mountain. The entire festival lasted almost two months.

On your way back to the car park, you can stop to buy fresh fruit. Do try the *salak*, also known as snakeskin fruit, which is grown in the vicinity.

If you have had enough of sightseeing for the day, return by the same route via Klungkung. Otherwise, make a picturesque, albeit time-consuming detour, via Selat and Putung to the east coast at Candidasa. With stops, it should take about two hours to reach Candidasa, where you can spend the night. To follow this route, turn left near the restaurant car park. The road leads through *salak* plantations, little villages and magnificent rice terraces. Don't miss the turn to ★★★**Putung near Rendang**. This

An assortment of fruit

Restaurant and view, Putung Bungalows

stretch of road is a must-see attraction for every visitor to Bali. A good place to stop for lunch is the restaurant at the Putung Bungalows, a small *losmen* near the village of the same name. The spicy fish prepared in banana leaves (*ikan pepes à la Putung*) is as excellent as the view stretching across rice terraces and coconut groves to the blue waves of the Indian Ocean and Nusa Penida island offshore.

The restaurant is also the starting point for one of the loveliest walks on Bali, linking Putung with the village of Manggis near the coast. If you have taken a car with a driver, you can ask him to wait for you in Manggis near the exclusive accommodation Griya Wisata. The path continues straight ahead and runs gently downhill (remember to wear suitable shoes). After passing through *salak* plantations it continues through rice terraces with a constantly changing panorama of spectacular views. After about two hours you will reach your rendezvous, where you can enjoy refreshments in the Griya Wisata.

Walkers will be disappointed to hear that the path is asphalted, but local farmers, needed roads and communications. The paved path has shortened the journey to Candidasa considerably.

The route continues through Bungaya and Prasi, and eventually arrives in ★**Candidasa**. Until the early 1980s this little fishing village on a lovely bay began its transformation into a seaside resort to attract tourists away from the southern beaches. The first visitors to arrive were backpackers, but the quality of accommodation soon improved to meet more demanding tastes.

Today, there is hardly an empty plot of land along the beach – or rather, what is left of it. Dynamite fishing destroyed the protective coral reefs, so that nature now takes its revenge by washing away the sand. For several years, attempts have been made to prevent erosion by means of concrete walls. Some hotels have even started trying to replace the sand by the lorry load and have offer artificial alternatives – swimming pools.

Still smiling in Candidasa

Apart from the beach, Candidasa still is a pretty place with some attractive hotels and good seafood restaurants. It's a good base from which to explore the east coast. The further east you go, the less densely packed it is.

If you prefer not to continue along the eastern route to Singaraja, return to the south along the main road through Klungkung. The little village of ★**Padang Bai**, on a beautiful bay, boasts the island's only natural harbour. For many years it provided the only direct sea link with Lombok. Today, a ferry still leaves here for the neighbouring island three times daily, although fast boats also leave from Benoa (*see page 64*).

An area enclosed by white sand coves and turquoise sea, the small harbor makes a good place for visiting yachts. There are a few bed and breakfasts here and the beach is fine. The history of this coastal village is closely connected with Empu Kuturan who arrived here in the 11th Century. Kuturan was a priest of great stature and is remembered for his reforms of village organization.

About 3km (2 miles) past Padang Bai, is ★**Goa Lawah**, the 'Bat Cave' temple dedicated to the spirits of the underworld. The temple itself is of little artistic interest, although its origins can be traced back to the 11th century. Nonetheless, it is one of the royal temples and is regarded as the counterpart to Pura Besakih, the temple of heaven.

No one has ever gone inside the cave. Its entrance is also the inner temple courtyard, and legend has it that the cave leads all the way back to Besakih and may even continue to an underground river that supposedly comes up at Pura Goa within the Besakih complex.

The main attraction at Goa Lawah is the colony of bats – thousands of them – which seem permanently glued to the walls of the cave. Their presence accounts for the sweetish odour and the droppings which cover the temple shrines. The temple is held to be ruled by two cobra snakes, Basuki and Antaboga – who, providing they like bats, will never go hungry.

On the other side of the road is a black lava beach, a relic of the last eruption of Gunung Agung. Sea salt is extracted by primitive methods, providing a small extra income for the local fishermen and their families, whose brightly coloured outriggers line the beach. The best time of day to visit this particular area is at sunset, when the beach is bathed in a magical light and the local inhabitants gather round to chat.

49

Extracting salt, and Padang Bai at dusk

Excursions from Candidasa

Amlapura and the water palaces of the Rajas of Karangasem

After the disintegration of the rulers of the Gelgel/Klungkung dynasty, Karangasem developed during the 17th and 18th centuries into the most powerful principality on the island. Apart from governing Bali, its Rajas also partly ruled over the neighbouring Lombok island. The Golden Age of Karangasem continued when the Dutch occupied the island. Like the Raja of Gianyar, the Raja of Karangasem made a treaty with the colonial forces, but whilst the palaces of Badung and Klungkung were laid to ashes, the local Raja was able to retain not only his title but some of his power. Thus the royal family was able to maintain its elaborate court and indulge in its love of water palaces until World War II. However, these magnificent relics from the most glittering period of the region's history became victims of natural catastrophe when Gunung Agung erupted in 1963 (*see page 47*).

Take the main road out of Candidasa east for 20 minutes to reach the first of the Karangasem palaces.

Until the volcano erupted, the town of **Amlapura** bore the same name as the province, named after the ancient kingdom of Karangasem. After the catastrophe, as an optimistic indication of its new beginning, the town received its new name. The **Puri Agung Kanginan** has seen better days, but when it was built at the beginning of the 20th century it was considered to be one of the most magnificent palaces on the entire island. The various *bales* (pavilions) are grouped around an artificial lake and display an interesting hotchpotch of styles linking Balinese, European and Chinese elements.

Amlapura sunset

Four kilometres (3 miles) southeast of the provincial capital lies the fishing village of **Ujung**. The ruins of the water palace, which were damaged during the volcanic catastrophe of 1963, are in danger of being swallowed up by the surrounding vegetation, but you can still sense the former grandeur and magnificence of the complex. With a little imagination it is easy to picture the water-loving Raja bathing in his pleasure palace, surrounded by his companions.

Chess mates in Ujung

During the 1940s, as a contrast to his palace by the sea, the last Raja built another water palace on the slopes of Gunung Agung, 6km (4 miles) northwest of Amlapura. ★**Tirtagangga**, 'The Water of the Ganges', also was damaged by the eruption of Gunung Agung. However, the pools and fountains remain intact. Some of them have been restored, and one pool has been transformed into a public bathing pool. A dip in the cool spring water, fed by mountain streams and spouting out of fountains and stone animals, provides welcome relief from the heat before lunch in the palace restaurant. Visitors seeking respite from the bustle of Candidasa should stay at the Kusumajaya Inn, very basic accommodation but boasting a magnificent view of the surrounding rice terraces. Long walks across the fields provide a good opportunity to study the irrigation structures.

Tenganan

★★Tenganan is one of the few villages in Bali where the culture of the Bali Aga, the Old Balinese, is preserved. The village lies in the hills 3km (2 miles) north of Candidasa. Visitors without their own transport will be met on the approach road by motorbike taxis. The alternative is to take a scenic three-hour walk to the village, but be forewarned that only hardy walkers should attempt this. The road surface is very uneven in places and walkers face a fair amount of uphill and downhill trekking. The breathtaking views, more than compensate for the exertion. The path begins opposite the homestay in the centre of town.

The Tenganan region, covering an area of 350 hectares (865 acres), is divided into five districts and has a population of about 3,800. The true Bali Aga live in the village of Tenganan Pegeringsingan, whose population has remained constant at about 300 for many years. Until the 1970s, Tenganan was a closed society, visited only by the occasional ethnologist. An entrance fee is now charged, a sign that times have changed. Even at a distance, Tenganan looks different from other Balinese villages. Surrounded by a wall, it can be entered only through one of four gates. The homesteads line the village road, which leads up the mountain. In the middle are the community rooms and the assembly pavilions. The Tenganan peo-

The heart of rural Bali

51

Masks in Tenganan

ple are proud of their lineage, which they trace back to the god Indra. They have never adopted the caste system favoured by the other islanders and live according to the ancient traditions of the Bali Aga.

The village men of Tenganan traditionally own land, letting their property work for them and banking the profits, which guarantees a carefree life. In the past, private property was unknown, and the profits from the rice fields were shared amongst the inhabitants. Today, however, no mention is made of what happens to the profits from the various souvenir shops. Tourist money has changed the face of Tenganan. Visitors strolling along the village street past the endless rows of souvenir shops, may well ask themselves how long the elite society of Tenganan will survive, in view of the high price that the 'chosen ones' – as the villagers like to call themselves – must pay for their wealth.

Each village community member must submit himself to the traditional rules of society. From an early age, the children become members of boys' or girls' associations, through which they learn the basic precepts of the Bali Aga community. The strictest rule is endogamy, i.e. marriage only within the village community. Anyone taking a partner outside the village boundaries must live in the Street of Exiles at the far end of the village or even leave the village entirely. This rule keeps the land within the community. However, it leads to fertility problems and decreasing numbers of Tenganese.

Also world-famous is Tenganan's double *ikat* weaving technique. It is a highly complex procedure in which both warp and weft threads are dyed before the weaving process begins. The women who sit at the looms need a great deal of patience to fit the patterns together. Some of the cloths, reserved for ritual purposes, are the result of years of work. A single cloth can take up to five years to complete. It is no wonder that the next generation of weavers is in short supply. The cloths – known as *geringsing*, meaning 'repelling illness' because of their magical properties – are coveted items in Bali, and collectors will pay high prices for this precious fabric. A large piece can cost well over a thousand dollars. In souvenir shops, however, you often find inferior quality fabrics on sale at lower prices.

Another Balinese tradition has survived in Tenganan – the creation of *lontar* books. This involves painting the leaves of the lontar palm with Old Balinese texts and illustrations from the great Hindu epics. The task is generally undertaken by men, who inscribe the characters and pictures onto leaves previously soaked in a bath of plant extracts. The drawings are completed by means of a mixture of oil and rust.

Preparing for a fight in Tenganan

Lontar books are made of palm leaves

Route 7

Along the North Coast

**Candidasa – Amed – Tulamben – Kubutambahan –
Singaraja – Lovina Beach** *See map on pages 30–1*

Once visitors have been to the island's interior, they are
usually inspired to explore further north. This route, which
follows the sometimes wild and arid coast of eastern Bali
to the north of the island, takes you to undeveloped and
often charming places. Kubutambahan boasts a north
Balinese temple which is markedly different from all the
other temples on the island. Singaraja is the northern hub
and the Lovina beaches form the northern tourist centre.
The route, leading from Candidasa around the semicircular protrusion on the east coast to as far as Lovina
Beach covers a distance of 160km (100 miles). The
volcanic forces of fire and water power have created over
the centuries a unique and inaccessible coastal landscape
around Gunung Seraya (1,175m/3,760ft), which is largely
unknown to most tourists.

Gamelan band leader

53

Only experienced drivers who aren't fazed by the prospect
of travelling 50 hair-raising kilometres (31 miles) along
narrow and, in places, badly maintained roads with many
sharp bends, should consider exploring this section of
the route. The journey from Ujung to Amed will take up
to two hours. If it has rained hard, some of the streams that
must be crossed en route will have turn into miniature
rivers, representing an insurmountable obstacle, even with
four-wheel drive. Less adventurous drivers should take
the route through Tirtagangga (135km/84 miles from
Candidasa to Lovina).

Whether it is bright and sunny or rainy and gloomy, the
trip through the ★★**rice-terrace landscape** between
Candidasa and Amlapura is one of remarkable scenic
beauty. The harsh tropical weather of Bali has turned into
fertile soil, some of the streams of lava which flowed
across the countryside southeast of Karangasem during
the last eruption of Gunung Agung. Most people want to
make frequent photography stops or go for short walks
to more closely examine the skilled rice terraces architecture. One stop, in any case, is essential. As you drive
into Amlapura, stop at the Pertamina petrol station on
the right-hand side of the road. This is your last chance
to fill the car's fuel tank before Singaraja.

Remarkable rice terracing

Last chance to fill up

Just before the royal palace in Amlapura (*see page 50*)
is a turn on the right-hand side leading to Ujung. After you
have passed the water palace, the paddy fields peter out

Brightly painted prahus

Diving is popular at Tulamben

and give way to less fertile upland. Maize and vegetables are interspersed with occasional vines, and village life reflects the meagre natural resources. Most visitors are fascinated by the austere beauty of the coastal scenery. The volcanic debris deposited on the eastern coast of the island creates a semicircular protuberance where the deeply cleft mountain slopes plunge down to the sea to form a succession of bays. Around almost every bend, another spectacular view of the valleys and bays opens up, the water's edge fringed by a line of brightly painted *prahus* (outriggers). Shortly before you reach the fishing village of **Amed**, you will come to **Lipah beach**, where the Hidden Paradise Cottages (*see page 100*) make a pleasant place to stop before continuing the journey to **Culik**. Here you should turn off to the north.

The most tiring part of the journey is now over, and the route continues along a well maintained road through landscape interspersed with outcrops of rock. At **Tulamben**, the scenery drastically changes to dry hills covered with scrub. This beach here is a favourite with water sports enthusiasts. The main pastimes are diving and snorkelling around the wreck of the *USS Liberty* which sank in the waters here during World War II. Apart from that there is little else of interest.

The northeastern coast road continues through the sparsely populated, austere, coastal lowlands. It seems surprising that a tropical island like Bali should possess such an arid region. Scrubland gives way to lontar palm trees, with the occasional field of dry crops such as maize, soy beans and peanuts. The road crosses a number of dried-out watercourses and is bounded by stone walls on which a few cacti grow. During the monsoon season, the lava gullies fill with streams of water from Gunung Agung's northern flank. Depending on the weather and time of day, the volcano appears to rise majestically above the countryside or disappears behind a curtain of clouds. A popular stopover is **Sambirenteng**, where the Alam Anda Bungalows provide a congenial overnight stay (*see page 101*).

As you continue towards **Air Sanih**, the northern foothills of Gunung Penulisan are covered with thick vegetation. The spring water pool on the right-hand side of the road provides an opportunity for a refreshing swim. Simple accommodation and a restaurant are available here.

Kubutambahan, the next stop, is the nearest you get to the northern tip of the island. In the centre of the village, on the right-hand side of the street, stands the ★**Pura Meduwe Karang**. Spread across three terraces, the temple is very different in style from those found in southern Bali. As well as the *Trimurti* (Brahma, Vishnu and Shiva), the 'Lord of the Fields' is worshipped here. He

Stone walls support cacti

is the masculine equivalent of the rice goddess Dewi Sri and watches over the coffee and maize crops in the region. The temple also has its army of guardians in the form of young boys, who will probably greet you on the steps leading up to the first terrace in order to guide you to the famous motif of the lotus bicycle on the northern perimeter wall. The bicycle's wheel and cog are depicted as stone flowers, while a real frangipani blossom often adorns the cyclist's carved ear, said to be a rendition of W.O.J. Nieuwenkamp, a Dutch archaeologist who travelled around the island at the turn of the century on a bicycle. Also of interest is the *Trimurti* carved in the base of the central terrace. Other reliefs depict a legong dancer and rural scenes like that of a farmer ploughing the field.

Pura Meduwe Karang

About 8km (5 miles) before Singaraja, in the village of **Sangsit**, is the **Pura Beji**. Built in the 15th century and dedicated to the rice goddess Dewi Sri, this temple is adorned with numerous *nagas* (serpents), which are symbols of fertility. The local *subak*, the association which manages the water needed to irrigate the rice fields, is responsible for the upkeep of this temple.

55

The route continues to ★**Singaraja**. With a population of some 566,000 inhabitants, this town is the commercial centre of the north as well as the administrative capital of the district of Buleleng. The town was of great importance in the late 19th century when Bali was under Dutch colonial rule, and until 1945 it was the capital of Bali. Today, Singaraja has lost its political and economic significance. The **Gedung Kirtya Library** on Jalan Veteran houses a collection of almost 3,000 *lontar* books, which record the island's history, literature, legends and religious practices on preserved palm leaves. They include the oldest written documents on the island and are

Pura Meduwe Karang: the cyclist

important for scientific research rather than items of interest to the casual visitor. Singaraja also is worth exploring at night. After dark the streets fill with life, with the **night market** turning into a centre of activity and the aroma of freshly grilled satay wafting around the stalls.

The route continues along the main road toward Gilimanuk, crosses the fertile coastal plain and, after another 10km (6 miles), reaches **Lovina Beach**. Several

Lovina Beach

villages form the hub of a number of tourist enclaves which are strung along the coast. The black lava beaches and their murky waters can't be compared with those in the south, but the region is ideal for visitors in search of peace and relaxation. There is some good snorkelling on the offshore reef, but those who prefer to stay dry can take a boat trip to see the dolphins which swim along the coast. The charming mountain scenery in the vicinity will encourage you to explore the area on foot, while the beach is ideal for a gentle stroll. There are numerous *losmens* (guesthouses) and mid-range hotels and resorts for visitors planning a longer stay.

Excursions from Lovina Beach

Lake Bratan

Brahma Vihara Monastery

On the way to Lake Bratan, stop to visit the **Brahma Vihara Monastery**. From Lovina, turn towards Banjar just before Seririt. The monastery is situated high on a hill just south of Banjar and has lovely views. Inhabited by a single Buddhist monk, the complex is spread out across a terrace around a lotus pond. The paintings on the wall of the main hall relate episodes from the life of Buddha, worshipped by Bali's Chinese population.

The two-hour drive to the lake along a winding, minor road, passes through dramatically beautiful mountain scenery. In Seririt is a turn on the left-hand side leading to Pupuan and Denpasar. A few kilometres further, in the village of Mayong, take the road signposted to Munduk. Passing between rice fields, the road slowly climbs into the mountains, offering breathtaking views of the steep valleys cutting through the cloud-covered volcanoes. The coast gradually retreats and, between Kayuputih and Munduk, the narrow road meanders between dense hedges of coffee, cocoa and vanilla plantations growing in the shade of a forest of lofty clove trees. Shortly after entering **Munduk** village, you may break your journey at the Puri Lumbung Bungalow complex or spend the night (*see page 100*).

Lake Tamblingan and **Lake Buyan** lie a short distance further on, close together on the right-hand side below the road. Because of the higher altitude, temperatures are much cooler here than the coast, giving the whole area an alpine feel. You shortly come to the main road which

links the north and south of the island, running along the west bank of ★★**Lake Bratan**. Nestling amongst the cloud-covered forests, this mysterious lake is said to be the home of Dewi Danu, the goddess of the lake. She is worshipped in the spectacularly located ★★**Pura Ulun Danu**, where two shrines seem to rise from the waters. Set against beautifully landscaped gardens, the temple was built in 1633 by the Raja of Mengwi.

Lakes Buyan and Tamblingan

Pura Ulun Danu

On the lake is **Bedugul**, a small town which has given its name to this entire mountain lake area, long-used as a weekend retreat by the Balinese. Nearby **Candi Kuning** boasts a wonderfully colourful spice, fruit and orchid market, which will leave a vivid impression of the cornucopia of tropical flora of Bali. For those wishing to spend a night here, the Ashram Guesthouse offers cosy lakeview rooms (*see page 99*).

Local flora at the market

Menjangan

Also known as Deer Island, **Menjangan** is an arid island off the northwest coast of Bali. It is part of the Bali Barat National Park (*see page 86*) and is a popular destination for diving and snorkelling enthusiasts. The island is uninhabited except for the Java deer and overnight stays are prohibited by the national park authorities. You can book an organised day trip in Lovina through one of the diving operators (*see page 85*). Alternatively, your hotel in Lovina also may arrange similar excursions. Don't forget your passport, as all visitors to the national park must register.

If you are exploring the north coast of Bali and want to stop for a night or two, you should turn off to the right a few kilometres after the Pulaki Temple in Pemuteran. The signs to Pondok Sari will lead you to the pretty bungalow complex (*see page 100*).

Route 8

Baroque temples and austere scenery

Sidan – Bangli – Penelokan – Gunung Batur – Pura
Jagaraga – Singaraja – Lovina *See map on pages 30–1*

The journey to the north offers a chance to see yet more
Balinese temples and experience the island's spectacular scenery. An alternative to the route described here is to
follow the shorter route via Lake Bratan (*see page 57*).
Allow sufficient time to visit the less frequented temples
and for the relatively easy ascent of Gunung Batur. Toya
Bungkah is a convenient starting point for Gunung Batur,
while Lovina makes a good base for a restful holiday.
Follow the main road to Klungkung, the turn to Bangli and
Kintamani is left as you drive through Peteluan, a few
kilometres east of the regional capital, Gianyar. Traffic
conditions are less crowded here than on the east of the
island, and your enjoyment will increase as you approach
the highlands.

Pura Dalem Sidan

After about 2 km (3 miles) you reach ★**Pura Dalem
Sidan**, the 'Temple of the Dead'. The complex lies on a
right-hand bend and is a spectacular sight. The temple
architecture recalls that of northern Bali and the elaborate decorations reveal a remarkable attention to detail.
Dramatic portraits of Rangda with long, flame-like tongues
adorn the split gate. In front of the external perimeter wall
are a number of elaborate sculptures of fabulous creatures
and monsters, such as the fat demon resting his arm on the
sole of his foot. The temples most important architectural element is the magnificent covered gate, surrounded
by a stone border and appearing to stand in the midst of
a ring of fire. Its harmonious *candi* shape recalls Mount
Mahameru. The gate is flanked by two guardian Rangda
figures and a sculpture of the Durga which has just conquered the buffalo demon in human form. Balinese temples of the dead are always dedicated to Durga and Shiva
(*see page 69*).

Rural idyll near Sidan

Continuing through the fertile paddy fields and a succession of apparently prosperous villages, the road climbs
steadily towards **Bangli**. This neat and tidy capital of the
administrative region of the same name once was the centre of the Kingdom of Bangli and has managed to retain
its charming rural atmosphere.

The ★★**Pura Kehen** is the religious heart of the town's
many temples. It lies on the northern edge of the central
area, to the east of the main road to Kintamani. This 'Temple of the Treasury' is one of the largest religious com-

plexes on Bali. The first courtyard's origins can be traced back to the 11th century. It was constructed as a symbol of Mount Mahameru, the 'world mountain' (*see page 70*). It contains an enormous banyan tree and a *kulkul* tower. An attractively decorated *kori agung* (covered gate), leads to the first courtyard, while the *candi bentar* (split gate) serves as entrance to the second. Look for the plates adorning the terrace wall leading to the *jeroan*. The Chinese porcelain used to decorate the temple was considered very valuable as it was imported from abroad: some plates have been damaged or stolen and subsequently replaced.

Pura Kehen in Bangli

The 11-tiered *meru* is dedicated to Shiva and contains the temple treasures. It stands on the back of the tortoise Bedawang, which is entwined with two *nagas* (serpants). The construction provides an analogy of the Balinese conception of the universe, with the tortoise representing the Underworld, the main body of the shrine the Middle World, and the 11-tiered pagoda roof the Upper World. The *padmasana* (lotus throne) is an impressive piece of work with fine representations of various deities. During temple festivals, the throne is reserved as the seat of honour for the guests from the Upper World.

59

The next section of the road is well maintained but relatively little used. After 25km (16 miles), the road winds uphill towards Batur and paddy fields gradually give way to bamboo groves, vegetables and clove plantations. The vegetation is less luxuriant as the climate is cooler here. Driving through the villages you will be reminded that conditions here are harsher than in the lowlands, as the settlements are more scattered. If visibility is good, as you enter ★★Penelokan ('Place of the View'), you will have a breathtaking view of ★Gunung Batur (1,717m/

Pura Kehen – Temple of the Treasury

Ascending Gunung Batur

5,633ft), revered by the Balinese as the second most holy mountain on the island. The slopes of this still active volcano are covered by extensive fields of black lava which extend far down into the massive caldera. The basin-shaped valley, formed millions of years ago, contains Gunung Batur itself and the lake of the same name. On the southeastern shore of the lake stands Gunung Abang (2,153m/7,064ft). Its summit forms the highest point of the cauldron.

Visitors wishing to climb Gunung Batur should drive down to **Toya Bungkah**, about half an hour further. The village lies on the lake's western shore. Along the way the route is dotted with outcrops of lava left during the volcano's last eruption in 1963. A hotel provides a comfortable alternative to the simple *losmen* in the village. You may be tempted to go for a swim in the hot springs (*air panas*), especially on your return from Gunung Batur. However, there are no changing facilities here. On the opposite shore of the lake is the Bali Aga village of Trunyan (*see page 12*). Unfortunately, visitors are not welcome here.

Get up very early the next day – 4am at the latest – if you want to witness dawn on the summit of Gunung Batur. The path is clearly marked and you will need neither a guide nor a mountaineer's physique. Stout shoes are a must, as the upper slopes consist of sharp-edged lava stones and dust.

Trekkers who are reasonably fit need between four and five hours, including a leisurely pause for breakfast, to reach the summit and return. If it is raining, even experienced walkers should think carefully before setting out as the path will be slippery and possibly even hazardous. Anyway, under such conditions, the sunrise will be a washout.

Toya Bungkah

Back in Penelokan, continue along the crater rim (caldera) through Kintamani to **Penulisan**, where more than 300 steps lead up to the highest temple on the island. ★★**Pura Tegeh Koripan** on Gunung Penulisan (1,745m/5,725ft) consists of two simple courtyards which are not adorned with the usual *meru*. Instead there are numerous pavilions housing a large collection of stone sculptures. They represent various deities, including two well-preserved portraits of Ganesha, and former rulers. In some cases, the items can be traced back more than 1,000 years. The origin, age and purpose of some sculptures have not yet been determined. Some bear the *linggam-yoni* motif which symbolises the duality of male and female characteristics. The temple affords a fine view of the two sacred mountains Gunung Agung and Gunung Batur. On a clear day you can even see as far as Gunung Rinjani on Lombok.

Pura Tegeh Koripan also marks the highest point on the road, which then winds its way down through cloud-covered pine forests over a distance of 32km (20 miles) back to Singaraja. Rushing torrents filled by the frequent mountain rains accompany the road on its way. As the route continues away from the summit winding its way down, it offers glimpses of the coast once again. The horizon, bathed in light, forms a stark contrast to the cloudy skies above the mountains.

61

The route continues westwards from Kubutambahan, passing the Pura Meduwe Karang (*see page 55*). Just before the village of Sangsit, take the left fork to **Sawan**.

Growing up in Jagaraga

Halfway along this stretch is the ★**Pura Jagaraga**. The sculpted shapes and wealth of decorations make this temple one of the masterpieces of north Balinese religious architecture. The gate, which is unusually broad and therefore appears out of proportion, and the walls of this 'Temple of the Underworld' (*pura dalem*) are covered with ornamental detail best described as Balinese baroque. The carved stone figures seem to caricature certain details of physiognomy, with goggle-eyed demons and Rangdas with pendulous breasts and elongated fingers looking as if they had just stepped out of a cartoon.

Even more astounding, and humorous, are the reliefs on either side of the exterior wall. The central characters are white foreigners who represent a threat to the islanders. Expect to see scenes like those of two Europeans in a Model T Ford being held up by bandits, flying aces in aircraft plunging into the sea, and a Dutch steamer signalling an SOS when it is suddenly attacked by sea monsters. The scenes are a thought-provoking allegory of the Balinese fears of the world of the white man.

Thought-provoking relief at Jagaraga

Continue to Lovina Beach where overnight accommodation can be found (*see page 100*).

Route 9

The rice terraces of Pupuan

Lovina Beach – Pupuan – Antosari – South Bali *See map on pages 30–1*

The route via Pupuan is one of the most attractive of the roads that link the south and the north of the island. The trip from Lovina Beach through the sparsely populated western interior of Bali to Denpasar is about 100km (60 miles). Because of the area's relative isolation, the luxuriance of the tropical vegetation and the fertility of the island become all the more impressive. The route also passes through Bali's only wine-growing area, which lies near Lovina on the fertile coastal strip.

Encounters on the road to Pupuan

The main coast road towards Gilimanuk branches in Seririt to Pupuan and Denpasar. If you wish to bathe in the nearby hot springs, **Air Panas** (the route is signposted), continue through Tangguwesia and rejoin the main route at Pengastulan. From Busungbiyu, the scenery becomes progressively more dramatic.

You also can make a detour to see the **Brahma Vihara** monastery (*see page 56*). In this case, take the turning to Banjar just before entering Seririt. The monastery is situated just south of the village.

Continuing along the road to **Pupuan**, the route is accompanied by a series of breathtaking ★★views. Many visitors park their cars at the side of the road and get out to take a short walk or photograph the scenery. The steeply terraced rice fields are overwhelmingly beautiful as they plunge down the hillside in places like precipitous canyons. You can clearly make out the course taken by the irrigation water as it flows along rivers or lined canals, passing from the higher to the lower terraces. The Balinese genius is evident in these masterpieces of hydraulic engineering. On the upper slopes the rice terraces give way to *salak*, banana and clove plantations. South of Pupuan, the road gradually descends before winding westwards across the western foothills of Gunung Batukau. The volcano's summit is usually covered in clouds during the afternoon as you drive pass coffee and coconut plantations.

Copra by the roadside

By the roadside you will notice collection points for copra. The shelled coconuts are transported to Java, where the flesh is extracted and used as an ingredient in traditional Indonesian cosmetics. The shells are taken to Tabanan, where they are processed into the fibrous mats used as roofing material.

In Antosari the road rejoins the main route to Denpasar and the more populated tourist centres of the coast.

Route 10

Lombok

The neighbouring island of Lombok lies to the east of Bali, across the Strait of Lombok. Passing through this narrow stretch of ocean (35km/22 miles wide and 300m/984ft deep) is the famous Wallace Line (*see page 6*). The island also belongs to the Lesser Sundas group and covers an area of 4,600sq km (1,776sq miles). The geographical contrasts between the north and south of the island are remarkable. Surrounding Gunung Rinjani, one of the highest mountains in Indonesia (3,726m/12,224ft), the northern half of the island is crossed by a chain of mountains largely clothed with impenetrable teak forests. The population of this remote area is correspondingly sparse.

The agriculturally useful land in Lombok lies in the highlands and the adjoining fertile areas run from the more densely populated western region towards the east. The arid coastal lowlands are covered with savannah-like vegetation. There is no industry on the island and conditions for rice farming are less favourable than on Bali as the climate is drier. The main agricultural products are manioc, onions and coconuts. Fishing and cattle farming also are important.

Some 94 percent of the island's 2.5 million inhabitants

Fishing boat at Senggigi

63

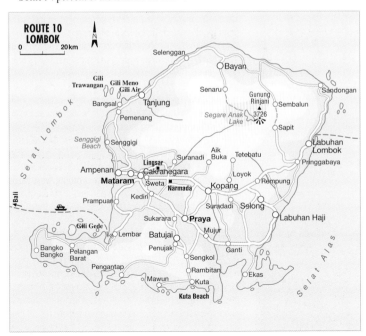

Sasak schoolboys

are Sasaks, thought to have originated from the mountain tribes of northwest India or Burma. They settled on Lombok earlier than the Malay immigrants. When Islam spread from Java into the eastern regions of the Indonesian archipelago, most of the Sasaks became Muslims. *Wetu-Telu*, the native religion of Lombok, which combines animism and ancestor worship with Muslim elements, is still practised in the north. Chinese and Arabic ethnic groups on the island, the Balinese minority, account for the remaining population. The latter have retained their Hindu-Dharma faith. Their existence can be traced to the military campaigns of the Rajas of Karangasem, who conquered North and West Lombok at the beginning of the 17th century. The Balinese feudal supremacy here continued until 1894, when they were defeated by the Dutch.

Merpati Airlines has several flights each day between Denpasar and Lombok's capital city of Mataram for around us$20. A comfortable and quicker alternative to the usually overcrowded ferry from Padang Bai in Bali to Lembar in Lombok is the Mabua Express. This modern passenger ferry sails daily between Benoa (just north of Nusa Dua) and Lembar, the main port on Lombok. Ships depart from Benoa at 8am and 2pm, and from Lembar at 11am and 5.30pm. The crossing takes at least two hours and costs around us$20–25.

Lombok's north coast

★★**Senggigi Beach**, the main tourist centre on Lombok, lies on the west coast of the island, about an hour's drive from Lembar or 30 minutes from the Selaparang airport at Mataram. The resort extends for several kilometres along a magnificent beach. It offers lodgings of all kinds and is an ideal base for exploring the island. If you prefer not to drive, hire a car with driver for a couple of days.

A major attraction for snorkelling and diving enthusiasts are the three islands off the northwest coast of Lombok, ★★**Gili Air**, ★★**Gili Meno** and ★★**Gili Trawangan**. All have magnificent beaches and coral reefs. Day trips from Senggigi are available, or boats can be chartered in Bangsal harbour, which lies north of Senggigi. Numerous hotels and guesthouses are located on the islands, although these mostly consist of simple *losmen*.

Boat to Gili Air...
...a paradise for snorkellers

On the south coast of Lombok, accessible via Sukarara and Penujak (*see page 66*), lies ★**Kuta**. This quiet fishing village should not be confused with its famous counterpart of the same name on Bali. Visitors seeking relaxation, who are content with simple accommodation and restaurants, will feel at home. Putri Mandalika Beach, east of Kuta, has one hotel, Novotel Lombok, with plans for others.

Excursions on Lombok

Mataram, Ampenan and Cakranegara and environs

Mataram, the capital of Lombok, is the administrative centre for the province of West Nusa Tenggara. Together with the neighbouring towns of **Ampenan** and **Cakranegara**, Mataram forms a bustling urban area with a population of about 400,000. Ampenan is the quieter district, whilst Cakranegara is the business centre and is also the home of most of the Chinese merchants who dominate trade on the island.

65

Most of the interesting sights are centred in Cakranegara. Raja Agung Made Gege Ngurah established his royal capital here in 1744 and the town still boasts many 18th century landmarks. Cakranegara also has the biggest market on Lombok. In **Sweta**, on the eastern edge of Cakranegara, you will find not only vegetables, fruit and food of all kinds but also a wide variety of household goods and a reasonable selection of craft items.

Sweta market

Pura Meru lies on Jalan Selaparang, the main traffic thoroughfare in Cakranegara. Founded in 1720, it was extensively restored in the early 1990s. The inner section of the temple, which is divided into three sections, is dominated by three imposing *meru* (pagodas). Each of the 33 smaller shrines is cared for by a different Hindu community in Lombok. Its annual Pujawali festival, held over five days during the September or October full moon, is the biggest Balinese event in Lambok. **Puri Taman Mayura**, on the other side of the street, dates from the late 19th century. It is a pretty complex reminiscent of Bali's water palaces. In the middle of the lotus pond stands a pavilion known as the Bale Kampung which once housed the island's main court.

Pura Lingsar

Narmada: inside the palace

Sasak weaving at Sukarara

Some 10km (6 miles) northeast of Cakranegara is the oldest temple on Lombok. ★**Pura Lingsar** is a spacious complex built in 1714. It is regarded as the 'Mother Temple'. It serves as a joint place of worship for Hindus, Muslims and followers of the *Wetu-Telu*, one of the two main socio-religious groups among the Sasaks, the Malay race who have lived on Lombok for at least 2,000 years. At this temple even local Chinese, Buddhists, Christians and occasionally *Waktu-Lima* (the second main Sasak religious group) come to pray for prosperity, rainwater, fertility, health and general success. In October, before the start of the monsoon, Hindus and Muslims gather here to pray specifically for a good harvest. The northernmost section of the complex, which is on a higher level than the rest, is the *pura* for Hindus.

In the northwest stands the **Hyung Tunggal** shrine, which is aligned towards Gunung Agung, whilst the **Bhatara Gunung Rinjani** in the northeast is dedicated to Gunung Rinjani, the seat of the gods on Lombok. The adjoining area contains an eel pond which is used by the *Wetu-Telu*. The Muslims pray beyond the temple wall.

The water palace and temple of ★★**Narmada** is 12km (8 miles) to the east of Cakranegara and is one of the largest and best preserved complexes on the entire island. A Balinese prince had the palace built in 1805 for his mistress, naming it after a sacred river in India. Some pools are available for swimming (modest suits are required), and traditional dances are held weekly in Narmada's splendid gardens.

You also can detour to **Suranadi**, and can stop at the hotel of the same name, built by the Dutch, for a refreshing swim in the spring water pool. The town's Hindu shrine – which is actually a complex of three temples – has a

sacred spring-fed pool with four sacred eels (*ikan belut*). Visitors are welcome to feed them with hard-boiled eggs which are sold at nearby stands.

Sukarara, 25km (16 miles) southeast of Mataram, is the centre of the Sasak weaving trade. It is still a cottage industry, and visitors are invited to watch the women sitting at simple looms and weaving the fine cotton or silk *ikat* fabric using time-honoured methods. It is possible to buy *ikat* at 'Rinjani Handwoven' (Jalan Pejanggik), Cakranegara. *Ikat* is ideal for curtains, cushions and seat-covers etc.

Lombok pottery

  Penujak, another 10km (6 miles) further south, is well known for its pottery, especially the thick-walled unvarnished pots and dishes of dark clay. The **Lombok Pottery Centre** in Mataram (Jalan Sriwijaya IIIA 7) provides the best introduction to the distinctive Sasak pottery, including the products of other surrounding villages such as Banyumulek or Masbagik.

Rambitan roofs

  ★**Rambitan**, a little further south, is a typical Sasak village with houses on stilts and characteristic rice barns with arched horseshoe-shaped roofs. For a small donation you will be taken on a guided tour of the village.

67

Mount Rinjani

It is worth finding time to drive through the picturesque fields and rice terraces to the Lombok highlands. **Loyok** is a village of basket-makers, where workers can be observed making baskets and other items out of rattan and gambir grass. Another village, **Tetebatu**, enjoys an attractive location and a pleasantly cool climate as well as fine views of Gunung Rinjani, the sacred volcano. **Kotaraja**, just south of Tetebatu, produces some of the best handicrafts in Lombok.

Hardy trekkers with enough time on their hands should consider climbing ★★**Gunung Rinjani**. Many visitors who have done so consider this to be the highlight of their stay in Lombok. However, it takes three full days to hike up to the summit and back. In addition, having reached the top the mountain, with its beautiful caldera lake, the view is frequently shrouded by heavy clouds which sometimes take hours to clear.

The caldera of Gunung Rinjani

  The climb can be done either via the track at **Senaru** or **Sembalun Bumbung** villages, the latter being the more difficult route. Guides and equipment can be hired at these villages. The best time to do the climb is during the dry season between May and November when the paths are not slippery and the chances of cloud cover on the summit are fewer. Climbers should carry most of their provisions since they're scarce in the villages.

Temples

Bali is often described as the 'Island of Ten Thousand Temples'. This is an understatement rather than an exaggeration, for in fact there are almost 20,000 of them, not counting the innumerable family temples and ancestral shrines which belong to every Balinese home. Every village community has at least three main temples. Within the boundaries of each village and looking towards the mountain, is the Pura Puseh, the principal temple, whilst in the heart of the village will be found the Pura Desa, the village temple. Towards the sea, outside the village limits and not far from the cremation ground, will be the Pura Dalem, the temple of the underworld. This is a place of worship dedicated to Shiva, the destroyer and renewer, and his consort Durga, the goddess of the dead.

In addition to these temples, there are *banjar* and *subak* temples (*see pages 12–13*), royal temples belonging to the former realms of the princely rulers. Although the significance of each temple varies, they all serve more or less the same religious function. Unlike in Christian traditions, for instance, the Balinese do not meet in the *pura* for private prayer or take part in community religious services. Temples come to life only on certain festival days, when they are elaborately decorated to greet the gods.

Carving at Pura Dalem

69

The basic design of a Balinese temple always follows a set pattern. The temple complex is protected by a surrounding wall and is usually divided by three subsidiary walls into three courtyards, lying one behind the other and entered through gateways. These gateways always are the most elaborate part of the temple as they serve as symbols of transition from one existence to the next. The temple is entered on the sea side through the split gate (*candi bentar*), which embodies the division of the cosmos and the duality of human life.

Split gate at Pura Meduwe Karang

Behind the gate is the outer courtyard (*jaba sisi*). This is a place of assembly after arriving in the temple, and symbolises the earthly realm. It contains a number of *bale*, roofed, open-sided pavilions where visitors can rest, and often a wooden signal drum (*kulkul*) on a platform or banyan tree. This also is where offerings are prepared during temple festival, and where the obligatory cockfight which marks the start of the festivities takes place. Cockfighting, unless part of a temple ceremony, is officially banned in Bali, but a collection of motorbikes by the roadside and a group of wildly gesticulating men usually indicate that a cockfight is in progress. This national sport has driven many families into ruin as gamblers sometimes stake even their homes on the outcome of a fight.

Pavilions at Pura Besakih

The temple's elaborately decorated covered gate (*kori agung*) leads to the middle courtyard. It is flanked by stone

Pura Taman Ayun
Bedulu, centre of early dynasties

guardian figures (*raksaka*) to frighten away demons wishing to enter. As a double protection, there often is another wall (*aling aling*) behind this entrance against which any evil spirits not deterred by the *raksaka* will crash into. According to Balinese lore, spirits cannot turn corners.

The middle courtyard, which prepares the faithful for their entrance into the holy of holies, houses a large assembly hall and pavilions where the gamelan instruments and cult objects used by the priests are stored.

The innermost gate provides access to the third courtyard (*jeroan*) which is reserved for the gods. The first thing you will notice are the pagoda-like shrines (*meru*), symbolising the universal Mount Mahameru, the home of the gods. The importance of the god to which the shrine is dedicated to determines the number of roofs (*tumpang*); usually there is an uneven number between three and 11. In accordance with his rank, the 11-roofed *tumpang* is reserved for Shiva alone.

The most important part of the third courtyard, however, is the stone lotus throne (*padmasana*), positioned with its back to Gunung Agung. During temple festivals, Shiva, in his form as the sun god Surya, takes up his position on the throne. Sometimes, however, Shiva is equated with the supreme deity Sang Hyang Widi Wasa. In this case the image of the latter will be found adorning the back of the throne. You sometimes also find a triple *padmasana* for the *trisakti*, the divine trinity of Brahma, Vishnu and Shiva.

Also found in the *jeroan* is a reception pavilion for gods who have no special place of honour within the temple, as well as a *bale* where food offerings are made, and at least one closed shrine in which the most sacred temple relics such as *lontar* books, *kris* (ceremonial swords) and masks are safely kept.

Food is offered at the bale

Festivals and Ceremonies

The *kulkul* drum reverberates three times – the gods have arrived. To honour their presence, the villagers have staged an elaborate festival in their temple, normally unused and unadorned on other days. The preparations last for several days during which the temples are decorated and the village streets bordered by flags on bent bamboo canes (*penjor*) which symbolise the holy mountain. Men and women don their best sarongs. In the temple kitchen, some of the men prepare the festive meal, the central dish made from the meat of sacrificed animals. The gamelan orchestra plays for the entertainment of the deities, and the air is heavy with the scent of frangipani blossoms and burning incense. The dance and drama which make up the entertainment delight gods and man alike and continue into the early morning hours.

The Balinese love festivities of all kinds, and hardly a day goes by without a temple festival being celebrated somewhere. In view of the vast number of temples, it's not surprising that the **Odalan** festival is the one most frequently celebrated. Every 210 days according to the Balinese *pawukon* calendar, the members of a temple community, be it village, district or just a single family, celebrate the anniversary of the temple's dedication.

Festival at Pura Besakih
Gamelan players

71

Another festival celebrated throughout the island is **Galungan**, which recalls the victory over the despotic demon princes. Pigs are slaughtered for offerings and ritual feasting. The faithful greet the gods and sacred ancestors on earth. Ten days later, during **Kuningan**, mortals take their leave of these same deities.

Apart from the *pawukon* calendar, the passage of time is also registered by another system, the *saka* calendar, introduced in AD78 when a famous Hindu saint arrived on Java from India. The date of the **Nyepi** festival, the Balinese New Year's celebration, is calculated by this calendar. On New Year's Eve, sumptuous offerings are presented to the powers of the underworld to lure them from their hiding places. At night, the islanders stay awake and make as much noise as possible using every imaginable instrument, in order to chase away the demons. The next day is devoted to prayer and meditation. No one is allowed to eat or to work, and at night no lamps may be lit and no lights switched on, so that any demons which venture back will think that the island is uninhabited. Even tourists are not permitted to leave the hotel on this day.

The Tourist Information Office produces a Calendar of Events listing the principal festivals.

Apart from these festivals, there are a number of private ceremonies, the so-called **rites of passage**, which

Dressed for the occasion

accompany a Balinese from the cradle to the grave. During pregnancy, the first offerings are made to the unborn child. Immediately after its birth, its 'four companions' (*kanda empat*) comprising umbilical cord, placenta, blood and amniotic fluid) must be buried. After 105 days another ceremony takes place during which the child is permitted to touch the ground for the first time. Until then, the body and soul of the child is regarded as too immature to come in contact with the realm of the demons. On its first birthday the child receives its name from the priest.

Another important ceremony marks puberty. This is the famous **tooth-filing ceremony**, during which the incisors and canine teeth are filed down slightly to symbolically eliminate demonic characteristics and to temper passions. To cut down on expenses, this occasion often is celebrated later when the children marry.

Balinese **marriage customs** are distinctive. The marriage is consummated before the wedding. The couple will plan for their honeymoon and stage the abduction of the bride. For the sake of propriety, the bride's parents will raise the alarm and start a search for their daughter, who by this time is spending her honeymoon in a secret place. About a week later the young couple reappears and begs the parents' forgiveness. The marriage must occur within 42 days of the kidnapping, before which a substantial dowry has to be paid by the groom's parents.

The most important festival, the one which takes place after a person's death. Since death is not seen as final, but simply as a transition from one existence into another – with any luck, a better one – the **cremation** ceremony

Guaranteeing a good send off

is a cause for celebration. It is, however, expensive, which is why Balinese cemeteries are full of temporarily buried bodies, awaiting to be cremated.

Mass cremations, in which a number of families share the costs, are the rule. Once the necessary funds are available, the priest will calculate a favourable date. Orders are placed for a cremation tower and an animal-shaped sarcophagus which form depends on the caste of the deceased. If already buried, the body is disinterred and the bones cleaned and arranged in the shape of a human body and draped with a white cloth. Relatives and friends arrive, and the cremation proper begins with a sumptuous feast. Afterwards, the corpse is placed on the tower, which is then brought to the cremation site near the Pura Dalem. On the way, the tower containing the body is turned several times in order to confuse the spirit, so that under no circumstances will it find its way home. At the cremation site the bones or corpse are transferred to the sarcophagus, which is then ignited. The ashes, the impure part of the deceased, are scattered on the sea, freeing the soul for its next existence.

Balinese Art

The casual young man in jeans who just raced past on his motorbike will appear a few minutes later in a traditional sarong as the member of a gamelan orchestra in the *banjar*. The manager of the little *losmen* in Ubud is also a gifted artist.

Bali is often described as an island of artists, and so it is all the more surprising to discover that the Balinese language has no term for 'artist' or 'art' as such. In former times there had been no need for such definitions. Until the dawn of the tourist era there were no professional artists on the island either. Even today, most Balinese continue to earn a living as rice farmers, but in their spare time many of them are also dancers, gamelan players, woodcarvers or painters – to the delight of the gods, as all these artistic activities are primarily performed in their honour first and as marketable commodities second.

Stonemasonry

Rangda's long tongue or the sharp claws of Kala greet the visitor in many temples. Comical or grotesque forms are the speciality of Balinese stonemasons, whose fantasy seems to know no bounds. While a classical severity dominates the the carvings of the south, in the north they are typified by an almost baroque voluptuousness. However, because the reliefs and sculptures are made of soft sandstone or volcanic tuff and weather quickly as a result of the high humidity, only a handful of ancient monuments still demonstrate these characteristics. The only exception is in the Pejeng district (*see pages 40–1*).

Buildings in Bali are not constructed for an eternity and no one is interested in creating works of art which will last forever. And if, today, you see concrete instead of carved stone ornaments adorning temples, it probably has more to do with cutting costs rather than durability. Similarly, when stone carvings are covered by green moss or lichen through age, they are simply replaced without a pang of sentiment by new statues which will give the gods just as much pleasure as the old ones.

Painting

In early times the Balinese painted on strips of canvas which were hung along the edge of temple roofs, or rectangular pieces of fabric which were used to decorate the palaces. The only famous method of painting was the *wayang* method, a style in which figures were depicted in a two-dimensional manner and in three-quarters profile, rather like those of the *wayang* shadow drama (*see page 77*). The themes were always drawn from mythology and only natural colours were used.

The art of the stonemason

73

Paintings adorn a temple roof

Following the arrival of the Dutch, there were no more commissioned works from the princely palaces and painting sank almost into oblivion. During the 1930s, however, an artistic revolution took place, due in no small part to the arrival of cultural refugees from Europe. Young artists began to experiment with modern materials from the West. Fabrics and natural colours were replaced by paper and canvas, oil and tempera paints. Pictures acquired the Western sense of perspective, and for the first time they were framed and signed, since individual works and not communal projects were being created. The subjects they portrayed were no longer purely religious but also illustrated everyday themes.

Artist at work

To contain the growing commercialisation while still offering gifted artists a chance to exhibit and sell their works, two European artists – Germany's Walter Spies (1895–1942) and Holland's Rudolf Bonnet (1895–1978) – together with Balinese Cokorde Sukawati – formed an artists' association known as Pita Maha. Within this group, various schools developed, including the Ubud and Batuan schools. A new generation of painters appeared in 1960 as the group Young Artists. In contrast to the Pita Maha school, these artists came from farming families and painted refreshingly non-academic works under the guidance of Arie Smit (born 1916), also from Holland. The centre of the artists' colony is still in Ubud (*see page 25*).

74

Woodcarving

At one time, wooden shrines, pillars and roof supports of temples and palaces were covered with reliefs and creepers which were brightly painted or covered with gold. Woodcarving was an art form that was always linked to architecture. Free-standing sculptures had little value, and were often restricted to masks. To this day, masks are

Intricate design at the Werdhi Budaya Art Centre

created by carvers who enjoy the same status as priests because they are considered to have magical powers. As in painting, centuries-old traditions were changed by the arrival of Europeans, under whose influence individual creative art began to develop. Not least for commercial reasons, they encouraged the Balinese woodcarvers to create free-standing sculptures which would appeal to tourist tastes. Accordingly, many of the sculptures today are just polished or subtly rather than garishly coloured. Clear lines are preferred to baroque shapes, and secular motifs appear alongside figures of deities.

A modern interpretation

An infinite variety of items is offered for sale in the countless galleries in Ubud and Mas. Mass production is being introduced, resulting in mediocre works. If you look hard enough, it still is possible to find original pieces. The craftsmanship of the items, usually carved out of tropical hardwoods, often is very good.

Metalwork

Goldsmiths and silversmiths have a long tradition in Bali. A visit to the workshops in Celuk (*see page 37*), for example, will provide an insight into the skills used to make jewellery and ornaments for Balinese women.

In former times the *kris*, a ceremonial sword, was a man's most valued possession. Even today, these weapons are proudly passed on from father to son. Long ago, the men who forged these swords held the same rank as priests and worked in accordance with a set ritual accompanied by magic formulas which gave the *kris* a religious importance. Few craftsmen have retained these ancient skills, and most weapons for sale in the island's souvenir shops today are derisively described as 'tourist daggers'.

Textiles

Whereas carving, painting and metalwork are still traditionally masculine skills, fabric weaving is a woman's domain. Particularly attractive are the intricately designed *songket* fabrics which uses gold and silver threads to produce sarongs for ceremonial occasions. *Ikat* weaving has become an art form throughout Indonesia, but *double ikat* is only produced in the village of Tenganan (*see page 52*).

Ikat thread and weaving

Batik is available in many shops, but it is mostly produced on Bali according to sketches created by Western designers. Manufacturers have stores in the Denpasar area. Both Balinese men and women buy *batik* in lengths of more than 2 metres, and wrap it untailored around the waist as a skirt-like *kamben* for traditional occasions. Like any other fabric, *batik* can range in quality. Bali's home-produced cloth, *endek*, is produced by hand on wooden looms and, when carefully tied and dyed, can hold its colours and prove more long-lasting than mass-produced cloths.

The classic pose

Music, Theatre and Dance

Gamelan orchestra

Music

At some stage during your holiday you are bound to hear a gamelan orchestra. These musicians, who accompany dance and theatrical performances, form an essential part of every festival. Almost every *banjar* (*see pages 12–13*) boasts its very own gamelan orchestra. The instruments are purchased jointly and are kept in the *bale gong*. Usually the orchestra consists of 30 to 40 men, although women's orchestras have become increasingly popular in recent times.

The name of the orchestra is derived from the word *gamel*, which means 'hammer' in Javanese and indicates the importance of percussion instruments in the band. Forming the centre of any gamelan orchestra are the big drums (*kendang*), which are always played by the leader of the orchestra. In addition, there are glockenspiels (*gender*), xylophones (*gambang*) and cymbals and gongs of various sizes. In some orchestras, there also are bamboo flutes (*suling*).

The musicians do not improvise, although to the uninitiated they may appear to be doing so. The gamelan troupe plays from memory since the Balinese have no system of musical notation. Various moods can be expressed with the help of two scales – the five-note scale *slendro* conveys the feeling of joy, while the seven-note *pelog* scale tends to sound more melancholy.

Each dance tells a story

Theatre and Dance

The great Hindu epics, *Ramayana* and the *Mahabharata*, which document the struggle between the forces of good and evil, pervade all Balinese thought. The stories, which span back thousands of years, were brought to southeast

Asia along with Hinduism. In Indonesia, the *Ramayana* and the *Mahabharata* have been part of the local folk tradition since the 11th century, when they were translated into the vernacular under King Airlangga. Every Balinese child knows the stories, and episodes are a perennially popular theme for many dance and theatre productions.

Wayang Kulit. The dramatic performances involving two-dimensional, artistic puppets cut out of buffalo hide in *wayang kulit* (*wayang* = shadow; *kulit* = hide or leather) originally served in pre-Hindu times as a religious ritual designed to establish contact with the ancestors. After the arrival of Hinduism, scenes from the *Ramayana* and *Mahabharata* provided the plot. *Wayang kulit* has been a popular art form ever since. It is, however, not just entertainment, nor is it just puppetry in the Western sense of the word, but rather a magical ritual to re-establish the cosmic order.

Wayang kulit puppets

Performed almost exclusively at major festivals, the entire *wayang kulit* performance stands or falls with one single man, the *dalang*. Having undergone lengthy training, he is much more than just a puppeteer and enjoys the same rank as a priest. Not only does he move the puppets, whose shadows are thrown onto the screen by a lamp, he also simultaneously undertakes all the speaking parts. Above all, the puppeteer must improvise and should be able to enliven the comic figures with political asides, or with references to local gossip.

77

Balinese dances and dance dramas have long been important advertisements for the 'Island of the Gods', but here – unlike elsewhere – they have not degenerated into a mere tourist spectacle. Bali's dance culture is more alive than ever, with almost every village having its own dance troupe and, thanks to income generated from tourism, they are now able to invest in new costumes, masks and ideas.

A break from the proceedings

Authentic dance performances usually are held at some ungodly hour and then only as part of a festival of several hours' duration. But visitors need not despair as the so-called tourist performances offer excerpts from several dances, and are usually of a very high standard.

All Balinese dances are by no means old. Some of the dance dramas date from pre-Hindu times, but many of the most famous ones were invented during the 19th century. New choreography constantly is being created. The roots of Balinese dance drama lie in the Hindu-Dharma faith, and to this day there are no clearly defined boundaries between religious practice, art and entertainment. Even if the character of the various dances seems profane, they are nonetheless performed as offerings to the gods within the framework of a temple festival.

To this day, the dancers are almost all amateurs, albeit with years of arduous training behind them. Would-be legong dancers, for example, start at the age of five. Generally, dancers specialise in one particular dance. Balinese dance usually revolves around a fixed repertoire of highly stylized and complex movements, based on the dance tradition of India. Only the comic characters have a certain amount of freedom to improvise.

Barong. This dance form, highly popular with tourists, is an exorcist ritual dating from animist times. It is stil performed in villages in times of crisis today, with the aim of driving out demons.

Barong is an exorcist ritual

The theme of the Barong is the ancient struggle between good and evil in the form of two mythological creatures. Barong, the representative of the power of good, is portrayed by two men who wear lion's masks. The opponent is the wicked witch Rangda. The framework of the story, based on the Indian epics, leads up to a dramatic duel. During the fight, Rangda puts a spell on the *kris* dancers who come to the assistance of the Barong, making them turn their swords onto themselves. In an authentic performance, the *kris* dancers enter a state of trance. However, Barong's magic powers makes the men invulnerable, so that no blood is shed. The battle finally ends in a draw, for in the Balinese cosmos good and evil belong together like day and night.

78

Kecak. The chanting of a choir of 100 men in black and white checked *saput*, a monotonous *ke-cak-ke-cak*, will send cold shivers down the spine of many spectators. The men form a circle which serves as the actual dance arena. Against the light of oil lamps, the dancers relate the story of Rama and Sita. The archaic effect is deceptive, and belies the fact that this is one of Bali's most recent dance forms. The choreography was the work of Walter Spies when he was searching for a dance interlude for the film *Island of the Demons*. He adapted the male choir (which here replaces the gamelan orchestra) from an ancient incantation ritual and combined it with scenes from the *Ramayana*. The result was one of the most impressive dances on the island.

Kecak: modern variation on an ancient theme

Following the Kecak, some groups perform the **Fire Dance**, during which a man dances, while in a trance, across glowing coconut shells. During performances for tourists, however, he merely imitates a trance.

Other dances. Almost every young Balinese girl dreams of becoming a **Legong** dancer. The dance career begins at an early age, and it comes to an early end with the onset of puberty and its associated loss of purity. In the case of tourist performances, these rules are not always strictly observed. The dance came into being during the 19th century at the princely courts. It tells the story of a princess who loses her way, finds refuge at the court of a king, and then resists his approaches. This most attractive of the female dances is always popular with the tourists. Since the Legong is not long enough to fill an entire evening, it is usually presented as part of a mixed programme of other dances.

Legong dancers start young

The selection almost always includes **Baris**, a dance performed by men and exalting the virtues of Balinese warriors. **Kebyar Duduk** is of more modern origins and describes the problems of adolescents. Its complicated movements are performed while seated and follow the choreography established during the 1920s by the famous dancer Mario (I Ketut Maria).

The **Oleg Tambulilingan** or 'Dance of the Bumble Bee' tells of the courting ritual of a pair of bumble bees and is a recent invention. The final number in an evening of dance is often the **Topeng**, a masked dance. There are a large number of masks, but a universal favourite is that of the *orang tua*, the mask of an old man whose awkward movements are parodied with gentle irony.

Topeng mask

Other dances include the **Ramayana Ballet**, a colourful and fascinating presentation of the *Ramayana* epic, which takes about 90 minutes. The **Joged Bumbung** is one of the few social dances on Bali. By means of a fan, a young dancer lures young men onto the dance floor and encourages them to join in.

Schedule of theatrical and dance performances

Barong	Batubulan, daily 9am; Ubud (Puri Saren), Friday 6.30pm
Kecak	Denpasar (Art Centre), daily 6.30pm; Ubud (Padang Tegal), Sunday 7.30pm
Kecak and Fire Dance	Bona, Sunday and Monday 7.30pm; Batubulan, daily 6pm
Legong	Peliatan (Peliatan Stage), Friday 6.30pm; Peliatan (Pura Dalem), Saturday 7.30pm; Ubud (Puri Saren), Monday 7.30pm
Ramayana Ballet	Ubud (Puri Saren), Tuesday 7.30pm
Wayang Kulit	Ubud (Oka Kartini), Sunday and Wednesday 8pm

Dance performances are also presented regularly in the larger hotels in the tourist centres, usually in conjunction with a buffet supper.

Food and Drink

A short stroll through the night markets of Denpasar or Singaraja will provide a sensory introduction to the delights of Balinese cuisine. At one corner, the aroma of freshly grilled satay comes wafting across, while at the next you are assailed by the overpowering smell of *durian*. Everywhere (and not just at the night market) the air is heavy with the sweet and spicy aroma of *kretek*, the ever popular Indonesian clove-scented cigarettes. With the major tourist centres offering a range of international restaurants – Italian pastas and Mexican fajitas are all the more tempting in such an exotic setting – and mobile street side *warungs* serving delicious local food, it is not too difficult to find a convenient alternative to the humdrum Western fare served at hotels.

An abundant variety of fruit

Balinese cuisine

The basis of every Indonesian or Balinese meal is rice. So central is it to daily life that the Indonesian language distinguishes four different words for *rice*. As far as food is concerned, the most important one you should know is *nasi*, or rice as it appears on the plate. It may appear as *nasi putih* (white rice) or *nasi goreng* (rice fried with vegetables, meat and/or eggs).

81

Rice is traditionally eaten with the right hand, although in modern Balinese homes and in restaurants it is eaten with a spoon grasped in the right hand and a fork in the left hand – the fork is used to shovel the food onto the spoon. When ordering rice and a variety of accompanying dishes, remember that all the food is served at the same time as they are meant to be eaten together. Each person helps themselves to a serving of steaming white rice and then to a little of each of the three or four dishes of meat or vegetables which are placed at the centre of the table for all to share. Do not swamp your plate with food at the beginning but keep helping yourself to a little more of the food as the meal progresses. *Nasi goreng*, however, is a one-dish meal and is usually eaten on its own.

Balinese food generally is hot and spicy, its flavour derived from a blend of fresh spices, garlic, turmeric, onions and fiery chillies. Fresh coconuts, either grated or squeezed for milk, add richness and tone down the fieriness of the food while fragrant roots and leaves give a dish its characteristic full-bodied aroma. To cater to unaccustomed Western palates, cooks in restaurants generally go easy with the chillies and spices.

Perennial favourites include *soto ayam* (chicken soup), *gado-gado* (braised vegetables with peanut sauce) and *satay* (tiny kebab-like skewers of meat prepared on a char-

Succulent satay

Vegetables galore

coal grill and served with a spicy-sweet peanut sauce). These specialities are all popular in Indonesia. A number of milder dishes have been borrowed from Chinese cuisine and are recommended for those with delicate stomachs: *cap cai* is a mixed vegetable dish and *mie goreng* is fried noodles. A side dish of *sambal*, made with red-hot chillies and shrimp paste, normally accompanies a meal and should be approached with caution.

The sway-back pig is a native of Bali, and pork in general is popular on the island – unlike the rest of the country, where the majority of the population is Muslim. *Babi guling* (roast suckling pig) is often served at banquets, as is *bebek betutu* (duck roasted in banana leaves). Along the coast, excellent seafood is available and is turned into delicious dishes.

Drinks and desserts

The Balinese drink water or hot tea with their meals. During the day in the tropical climate, these are often a better choice than the admittedly light local beer. Beer fans, however, are in no danger of dying of thirst on Bali, and wine drinkers can often choose between *brem* rice wine or local Holten rose. Imported wines are available in the larger restaurants and hotels. The trendy bars on Kuta serve margaritas, but you could try instead *tuak* (palm wine) as an aperitif or *arak* (brandy) as a digestif. On a hot day, fresh coconut milk is invigorating: as well as helping to settle an upset stomach, it tastes good and is an excellent thirst-quencher.

Tropical tastes and tangy desserts

The best dessert is a plate of tropical fruits. Apart from the more familiar fruits like bananas, pineapple, papaya, mangoes and passion fruit, there are such exotic delights as *salak* (snakeskin fruit), *rambutan*, jackfruit and mangosteen. An unforgettable experience is the infamous *durian*, which is said to stink like hell and taste like heaven. Try it at least once. Descriptions of the flavour range from strawberries and cream to overripe goat cheese. To round off your meal with something more calorific, order black rice pudding with coconut milk (*nasi hitam*) or fried bananas (*pisang goreng*). *Selamat makan* – bon appetit!

Restaurants

The following selections for the major tourist centres are listed according to three categories: $$$ = expensive; $$ = moderate; $ = inexpensive.

Candidasa (area code 0363)
$**Pandan Restaurant**, on the beach, serves a Balinese buffet. $$**Baluki**, on the outskirts, serves excellent fresh fish and seafood. Situated directly by the sea and is a magnificent setting from which to watch the sun go down.

$Chandra's is along the main street and is well known for its grilled fish. **$$T.J.'s Cafe** also along the main street, tel: 41540, is an attractive establishment with an imaginative menu. A counterpart to the more famous branch in Kuta.

Denpasar (area code 0361)
$Hong Kong, Jalan Gajah Mada, tel: 43485. It offers reasonably priced Chinese cuisine. **$Rumah Makan Polaris**, Jalan Sulauesi 40, tel: 222640, is located south of the market and offers good chicken and vegetables dishes. **$Rumah Makan Betty**, Jalan Sumatra, tel: 224502. Delicious home-cooked quality Indonesian food that is served in clean surroundings.

Kuta/Legian (area code 0361)
$$Aromas of Bali, Jalan Legian, Kuta. A chic café-restaurant with an excellent and imaginative menu for vegetarians. **$$Goa 2001**, Jalan Seminyak, Legian, tel: 731178. This popular nightspot is also a fashionable meeting place while its adjoining restaurant serves excellent seafood. **$$Poppies** Jalan Segara Batu Bolong (Poppies Lane 1), Kuta, tel: 751059. The hotel is undoubtedly a classic amongst the typical local bungalow complexes. The same can be applied to the adjoining garden restaurant which has an extensive menu of both Western and local dishes. Reservations recommended. **$$T.J.'s Mexican**, Gang Poppies I, Kuta, tel: 751093. This restaurant is highly recommended for tasty Mexican cuisine prepared with great Balinese flair. T.J.'s also offers great wake-me-up margaritas. **$$Warung Kopi**, Jalan Legian, Kuta, tel: 753602. This centrally located café-restaurant has a varied menu and also serves excellent cakes.

Poppies, the garden restaurant

83

Elegant dining

Lovina Beach (area code 0362)

$Khi Khi Seafood Restaurant, Kalibukbuk, tel: 41548. As the name suggests, seafood is the speciality here. The must-try here is the grilled fish with *sambal* sauce. **$$Biyu Nasak**, Lovina Beach, tel: 41176. Nouvelle cuisine, Bali style.

Nusa Dua (area code 0361)

$$Mentari Ming Garden, Jalan Pantai Mengiat, Bualu, tel: 772125. Delicious Chinese cuisine. A range of Indonesian and international fare can be had at **$$Galeria Nusa Dua** food court. The **Ole Ole** and **Pica Pica** stalls are among the best in the food court. **$$Rai Seafood Restaurant**, Jalan Pratama, Tanjung Benoa, tel: 772012. Good selection of fish and seafood served in comfortable surroundings.

Sanur

$Borneo, Jalan Pantai Sindhu 11. A small restaurant serving elegant Indonesian dishes. **$$Donald's Cafe & Bakery**, Jalan Danau Tamblingan. International cuisine and a good choice of cakes. **$Mango Bar & Restaurant**, Jalan Pantai Sindhu, tel: 288411. On the beachfront, the fish specialities here are excellent. **$$Trattoria Da Marco**, off Jalan Mertasari, tel: 288996. Good tasting Italian pastas and pizza.

Ubud (area code 0361)

$Bali Cafe. Off Monkey Forest Road near the sports field, tel: 975540. Good Indonesian and European dishes. **$$$Bebek**, Jalan Hanoman, diagonally opposite the Dewi Sri Bungalows, tel: 975489. A fashionable eating place with Balinese flair. Right on the edge of the rice fields. **$$Cafe Wayan**, Monkey Forest Road, tel: 975447. Interesting East-meets-West cuisine and a great selection of cakes. A must-try when in Ubud. **$$$Casa Luna**, Jalan Raya Ubud, tel: 96283. Diagonally opposite the Lotus Cafe, this restaurant is a meeting place for the expat community in Ubud. Cosmopolitan menu and unmistakable nouvelle cuisine. **$$Lotus Cafe**, Jalan Raya, tel: 975660. Traditional restaurant in the centre of town, with an enchanting lotus pond as a backdrop. The specialities range from Indonesian dishes to Italian nouvelle cuisine. **$$Murnis Warung**, Campuhan, by the bridge, tel: 975233. A legend on the culinary horizon of Ubud.

The Lotus Cafe

Lombok

$$Cafe Wayan, Jalan Raya Senggigi. A branch of the famous counterpart in Ubud, but this not as good. **$$Sunshine Restaurant**, Jalan Raya Senggigi. Excellent Indonesian cuisine, fish specialities, seafood.

One man and his board

Active Holidays

Diving and snorkelling

The reefs of Sanur, Candidasa and Lovina offer even beginners a chance to explore Bali's underwater world. Flippers and masks are available for hire in many hotels and *losmen* (guesthouses). The most spectacular diving and snorkelling area is found just off the island of Menjagan (*see page 57*), which forms part of the Bali Barat National Park. Diving excursions and courses can be booked through many water sports firms in the tourist centres. Baruna Sports at 300B Jalan Bypass Ngurah Rai, Kuta, tel: 0361-753820, and the Ena Dive Centre, 7 Jalan Tirta Ening 1, Sanur, tel: 0361-287945. Both have a comprehensive programme of courses and diving equipment.

Snorkelling on Gili Air Island

Surfing

Surfboard novices hurl themselves into the waves on Kuta Beach. Experts prefer the waves at Suluban, Canggu and Mendewi beaches. Surfing is reasonably good throughout the year and especially good from June to August. Surfboards can be rented inexpensively at Ulu's Shop in Jalan Bakungsari and at Amphibia Surf Shop at Jalan Legian in Kuta.

Rafting

The latest rage amongst the adventurous is white-water rafting on the Ayung River in Kedewatan near Ubud. Rafters can be picked up from their hotels along the south coast. The best time to raft is during the rainy season from November to March when the water levels are reasonably high. Information and reservations: Adventure Tours, Jalan Bypass Pesanggaran, tel: 0361-721480; Sobek, 56x Jalan Bypass Ngurah Rai, Sanur, tel: 0361-287059. Bookings can also be made through many hotels in Ubud.

Rafting is best during the rainy season

Out to the islands

Cruising

The options are many, from luxury catamarans to no-frills ketches. Try the *Wakalouka* (tel: 0361-484085), a sleek catamaran for cruises to Nusa Lembongan. The day cruise includes meals, drinks and hotel transfers. Another option is the *Bali Hai* (tel: 0361-720331), a motorised catamaran offering day cruises to Nusa Lembongan. *Spice Island Cruises* (tel: 0361-286283) offers three and four day cruises to Komodo Island.

Outrigger sailing

Jukungs, local outrigger sailboats made from hollow logs with carved bows to resemble crocodiles, are available for charter all along Sanur, Lovina and Kusamba beaches.

Mountain climbing and jungle walks

Both Gunung Agung and Gunung Batur can be climbed in a day's excursion. The starting points are Besakih and Toya Bungkah respectively. You need to be fit, and stout shoes are essential. For both trips you will need warm clothing. Take food along with you if you are climbing Gunung Agung. Mountain guides are not strictly necessary, but will make life easier. They can be hired in any one of the *losmen* at your starting point.

The trip to the top of Gunung Batur and back will take about four to five hours; Gunung Agung takes at least twice as long. To climb Gunung Rinjani on Lombok (*see page 67*) you will need about four days; take all equipment and food with you. Information regarding the expedition can be obtained in Senggigi.

Guided walks through jungle or rice paddies can be booked through Sobek or Adventure Tours (see 'Rafting' for addresses). Try also Bali Bird Walks, by long-time resident Victor Mason. Walks conducted on Saturday, Sun-

Guides give local insight

day, Tuesday and Friday at 9am. Get a copy of his book, *Insight Pocket Guide: Bali Bird Walks*, if you intend to scramble around on your own (tel: 0361-975009).

Bali Barat National Park

The park administrative office (Monday to Thursday 7am–2pm, Friday 7–11am, Saturday 7am–12.30pm, tel: 0365-540060) is located near Gillimanuk, the port of embarkation for ferries to Java. The office can issue entry permits and allocate guides for day trips into the western part of the park, including the offshore island of Menjangan, famous for its coral gardens (*see page 57*). Simple accommodation is available in the park. Those wishing to camp must be accompanied by a guide and should bring tent, sleeping bag and food (cooking equipment is available for hire).

Golf

The 18-hole golf course at the Bali Handara Country Club (tel: 0361-288944), located north of Lake Bratan in the cool mountains, is one of the loveliest in the world. Guest players are welcome. If you plan to stay longer here, you can check into the Bali Handara Kosaido Country Club. Another option is the 18-hole Bali Golf and Country Club at Nusa Dua (tel: 0361-771791). The New Le Meridien Nirwana, 18-hole Greg Norman-designed course is in the shadow of Tanah Lot (tel: 0361-810066).

Guest players are welcome

Cycling

Many hotels offer bicycles or even mountain bikes for hire. Organised tours are available through Sobek or Adventure Tours (see 'Rafting' for addresses).

Bicycles can be rented

Dancing

By prior arrangement Oka, a young Balinese dancer, teaches visitors the principles of Balinese dance. Ubud, Jalan Kajeng 25, tel: 0361-96277.

Meditation

Sessions are held every evening in the Meditation Shop at Jalan Wanara Wana (Monkey Forest Road), Ubud, tel: 0361-976206. One- to five-day courses are also offered.

Music

Courses in gamelan playing are available. Check with the Ganesha Bookshop on Jalan Raya in Ubud.

Cooking

Indonesian cookery courses are held in the restaurant Casa Luna in the centre of Ubud, tel: 0361-96283, in the Serai Hotel, tel: 0363-41011 or Sua Bali, tel: 0361-941050.

Getting There

By air

The international airport Ngurah Rai, 13km (8 miles) southwest of Denpasar, is served by daily flights from Jakarta, Yogyakarta, Surabaya and other points in Indonesia by the national airline Garuda and smaller domestic airlines like Merpati and Bouraq. Bali is well connected with international flights by Singapore Airlines from the US (Los Angeles, San Francisco and New York), Europe (London, Amsterdam, Frankfurt, Paris and Zurich), Australia (Sydney, Melbourne, Darwin and Perth), and Asia (Singapore, Tokyo and Hong Kong). Many airlines fly only as far as Jakarta, where you transfer to one of the several daily flights to Bali. The Tourist Information Office has a counter at the airport where rooms can be booked, and there are bureaux de change and a taxi stand.

Denpasar airport

An airport tax of Rp25,000 is charged on leaving the country, Rp11,000 for domestic flights. Most airlines require confirmation of flight reservations at least 72 hours prior to departure. Ask for the re-confirmation code.

89

By bus

Considerably more tiring is the overnight trip by air-conditioned express bus from Denpasar to Yogya or on to Jakarta. As it takes about 30 hours to get to Denpasar, the bus is best for the truly adventurous. There also are bus connections to other cities in Java. The ferry portion of the journey (the boat arrives at Gilimanuk on the western coast of Bali) is included in the price of the bus ticket. Some buses go directly to Kuta or Sanur, but most end up at Denpasar. In Bali, bus companies have their offices at Jalan Diponegero and Jalan Hasannudin in Denpasar.

By train

Trains are slower but ideal if you have the time. From Jakarta, take the train to Banyuwangi on Java's eastern tip where you catch the bus that takes you to Bali by ferry.

By sea

If travelling overland from Java, the ferry leaves Ketapang for Gilimanuk on the western coast of Bali, the trip taking about 30 minutes. From Lembar, Lombok, ferries run regularly to Padang Bai, near Candidasa in eastern Bali. An express catamaran service also plies between Lembar and Benoa in southeast Bali. For further information *see page 64*. Padang Bai is visited twice every month by the passenger ship *Kelimutu*, run by the state-owned shipping line Pelni. The ship covers a two-week circuit around established routes in the Indonesian archipelago. The Pelni office can be contacted at Benoa, tel: 721377.

The ferry at Padang Bai

Getting Around

From the airport

Taxis are available at the taxi counter, and rates are posted for cars with air-conditioning and without for trips to the various centres. The fare is paid at the counter. Refuse offers from touts and informal guides loitering at the airport. Major hotels and pre-arranged tours usually provide their own transport.

By bus and bemo

Public buses are cheap, if uncomfortable, with routes that do not pass through the main tourist centres. Much more efficient is the shuttle bus run by the Perama Tourist Service. These run several times a day on the main routes between the tourist centres. Tickets can be bought in many *losmen* and at travel agents in the main tourist areas.

Even cheaper is the *bemo*, a mini-van, which usually runs along a prearranged route but which has no set bus stops. To get out, make your presence known by calling out to the driver. To check on the fare, ask the other passengers and pay the *bemo* conductor the correct sum – otherwise, as a foreigner, you are likely to pay over the odds. In the tourist centres, public *bemos* can be chartered for the day or for a one-way trip to a specific destination.

Dokars can still be hired

Dokar

In Denpasar, Singaraja and Klungkung there are still horse-drawn carriages for hire. *Dokars* also appear in Kuta, where they are a tourist attraction.

Taxis

Taxis are only available in the tourist centres along the south coast. The fare must be negotiated before the trip (ask your hotel for advice). Elsewhere, a taxi – usually a minibus – is simply a hired car with driver, or a chartered *bemo*. They are usually rented for day trips. The price depends on the distance travelled but expect to pay about Rp5,000 for the hour and Rp50,000 for the day. Metered taxis charge the metered rate. Ensure the meter is turned on when you set off.

Cars and minibuses

International car rental firms have branches at some of the luxury hotels along the south coast. Local firms are plentiful and significantly cheaper. An international driving licence is not necessary. Vehicles are usually Suzuki jeeps or the larger Toyota Kijang. Depending on its condition, rental period and hirer's negotiating skills, a jeep will cost Rp70,000–115,000 a day (not inclusive of insurance) from a local firm. Before signing a rental agreement, test drive and check the vehicle's condition, especially the brakes.

In general, a rented car without a driver can be recommended only to experienced drivers. Indonesians drive on the left-hand side, but the crucial (unwritten) rule is the stronger always has priority. Some drivers resemble kamikaze pilots, which seems out of character given the gentle Balinese temperament. Chickens and dogs are active participants in the traffic mêlée and should be mercilessly hooted off the road. If you don't feel up to facing such traffic on holiday, pay a little more and negotiate for a car with a driver. If there are enough of you, rent a minibus with a driver.

As you step out of your hotel, you will be deluged with offers of car and minibus rental. The following companies can be recommended (all numbers area code 0361):

Avis, Jalan Uluwati 84, Jimbaran, tel: 701770 or Novotel, tel: 772239, Denpasar, tel: 771210

Toyota Rent-a-Car, 99 Jalan Raya Airport, tel: 751282

Bagus Car Rental, 1 Jalan Duyung, Sanur, tel: 287794

Mega Jaya, 78X Jalan Raya Kuta, tel: 753760

Surya Agung Dewata, 39 Jalan Raya Kuta, tel: 752866

Crash helmets are compulsory

Motorcycles

Rental agencies are found at all the tourist centres. Although this is an economical way to travel (expect to pay about Rp25,000 – 30,000 a day), the chance of a traffic accident significantly increases. Crash helmets are compulsory and must be provided by the rental firm. While riding is more adventurous, the greater risk of physical injury in an accident may outweigh any advantages.

In the south there are plenty of fuel stations run by the state-owned oil company Pertamina. In more remote areas, look for the sign 'Premium'. Try to avoid village kiosks with handpainted signs, as the quality of the fuel sold by these is sometimes dubious.

A variety of options

Facts for the Visitor

Travel documents

To enter Indonesia, visitors from 46 nations require only a return air ticket and a passport valid for at least six months from the planned date of departure. A two-month entry permit is granted automatically on arrival but this can't be extended. If you leave the country you are allowed to re-enter again the next day for another two months. Visitors from all other countries must obtain a one-month visa from their local Indonesian embassy or consulate. Business travellers intending to work in Bali require a visa.

Customs

Items for personal use, including film and video cameras, typewriters and binoculars, may be imported freely. Other allowances include 2 litres of alcoholic drinks, 200 cigarettes (50 cigars or 100g tobacco), a reasonable amount of perfume, and presents to a total value of US$250. There is a ban on the import of publications in Chinese script, pornographic materials, pre-recorded video cassettes, weapons, narcotics and fresh fruit.

Items more than 50 years old are classified as 'national treasures' and subject to export restrictions. Items which contravene the Washington Agreement on Endangered Species will be confiscated.

Tourist information

The local Tourist Information Office in Bali will supply information free of charge. Don't forget to ask for the Calendar of Events listing the main festivals. Information offices usually open Monday to Thursday 7am–2pm, Friday 8am–11am and Saturday 7am–12.30pm.

Denpasar: Badung Government Tourist Office, Jalan

Surapati 7, Denpasar, tel: (0361) 223602; Bali Government Tourist Office, Jalan S. Parman, Kompleks Niti Mandala, Renon, Denpasar, tel: (0361) 222387; **Kuta:** Tourist Information Centre, Jalan Raya Legian, tel: (0361) 753540; **Ubud:** Bina Wisata, Jalan Raya Ubud, tel: (0361) 96285, opposite the Pura Desa in the centre of town. Also sells tickets for dance performances and latest information e.g. on temple festivals (daily 8am–8.30pm); **Lombok:** Provincial Tourist Service, Jalan Langko 70, Ampenan, tel: (0370) 31829, 37828; Dept. of Tourism, Art and Culture, Jalan Singasari 2, tel: (0370) 32723.

In the UK: Indonesia Tourist Promotion Office, 3 Hanover Street, London W1R 9HH, tel: 0171-493 0030.

In the US: Indonesia Tourist Promotion Office, 3457 Wilshire Blvd, Los Angeles, CA 90010, tel: 213-387 2078.

In Southeast Asia: Indonesia Tourist Promotion Office, 10 Collyer Quay #15-07 Ocean Building, Singapore 0104, tel: (65) 534 2837.

Information kiosk

Currency and exchange

The Indonesian unit of currency is the Rupiah (Rp) and is available in notes of Rp100, 500, 1,000, 5,000, 10,000, 20,000 and 50,000. Coins are found in Rp25, 50, 100 and 500 denominations. It is wise to carry smaller notes especially in the remote areas as vendors may not carry enough change to break larger notes. The import and export of local currency is limited to 5 million. There are no restrictions concerning the import and export of foreign currency.

Money can be changed at banks (*see Opening Times*) and at licensed bureaux de change in the major tourist centres. The latter are open every day until late at night. Try to avoid changing money in hotels as the exchange rate is not so favourable.

Some Indonesian Rupiah

Visitors should take a supply of traveller's cheques in US$. MasterCard and Visa credit cards are accepted by the larger hotels and many art galleries; the American Express charge card, however, is not so widely accepted. The remaining Indonesian currency you have at the end of your holiday can be changed back at the airport if you present the relevant certificate of exchange.

Tipping

Tipping is alien to Indonesian culture, but this is slowly changing as a result of increased tourism. Today, waiters in top hotels and restaurants expect a tip of about 10 percent. They expect the tip even if a service charge is already added to the bill. Porters expect at least Rp500 per item of luggage. Chambermaids and taxi drivers, too, will be pleased to receive a small tip.

Shopping

Bright colours abound

Family business

It is not easy to curb one's enthusiasm for shopping in Bali. In Mas you will be tempted by woodcarvings, in Celuk by silverware, in Ubud by the famous paintings, and in Tenganan by fabrics and items made from lontar leaves. Cheap summer clothes can be bought everywhere, and the souvenir stands in the tourist centres are piled high with crafts of all kinds.

In the tourist centres, you will often be surrounded by traders of every kind. Attempt to affect disinterest and try, above all, to remain friendly, even if it is difficult to do so. Remember that the salesmen are just trying to earn a living. Bargaining is the norm in markets, smaller shops and art galleries, although it is considered good manners not to fight for the last penny. Increasing numbers of boutiques are adopting a fixed-price policy.

When buying souvenirs, check on export regulations. Any item which is over 50 years old is classified as an antique and its export is restricted. It is also prudent to remember that the Washington Agreement prohibits the import of certain goods, e.g. those made with ivory, tortoiseshell and snakeskin, into Europe and the US.

Opening times

Banks: Monday to Friday 8am–3pm; Saturday 8–11am.
Shops: most are open daily until 9 or 10pm.
Government offices: Monday to Thursday 8am–2pm, Friday 8am–11am, Saturday 8am–12 noon.

Public holidays

Official holidays: 1 January (New Year); 17 August (Independence Day); 25 December (Christmas)
Semi-official holidays: 21 April (Kartini Day - Women's Day); 1 October (Pancasila Day – Constitution Day), 5 October (Armed Forces Day)

The various religious holidays are too numerous to list. Their dates vary from year to year as they are calculated according to the *Pawukon* or *Saka* calendars. The Tourist Information Office produces a *Calendar of Events* which lists the various dates for the coming year.

Postal services

Post offices (*Kantor Pos dan Giro*) in Denpasar and major towns are usually open from Monday to Thursday 8am–2pm, on Friday 8–11am and on Saturday 8am–12.30pm. Stamps can also be bought from the postal services counters in the tourist centres and in many hotels. Mail to Europe and the US takes about 10 days, air parcels take between two to three weeks, sea parcels about three months. There are numerous reliable cargo firms in the various tourist centres.

Telephones

Indonesia's telephone network is usually overloaded. You will need patience if you plan to use a public call box and a large supply of Rp100 coins. Card telephones are becoming more frequent. International direct dialling is available at telecommunications offices (*Wartel*) at the major tourist centres, and hotels, although the charges levied by the latter are frequently very high. Many hotels have card phones and provide phone cards at reception. For international calls, dial 001 or 008, then the country code and the number itself.

Guaranteed delivery

Time

Indonesia has three time zones. Bali and Lombok both use Central Indonesian Time, which is GMT + 8 hours. During the summer months the time difference is + 7 hours.

Electricity

Voltage is generally 220V but a few places still operate on 100V. While adapters are available for loan in better hotels, it's advisable you bring the appropriate one along.

Medical

Only vaccination required is against yellow fever for visitors arriving from an infected area.

Before leaving for Bali, it is advisable to ask your doctor or local Institute of Tropical Medicine whether malaria prophylaxis is necessary. You should also ensure that you have a valid vaccination against polio and tetanus. Also recommended is the gamma globulin injection for protection against hepatitis A.

The usual medicines are available in pharmacies (*apotik*) and are generally available without prescription. However, take a supply of frequently needed items. Preparations for the treatment of diarrhoea, sunburn and colds should be included. Local preparations are often the most effective against insect bites (ask in your hotel).

Observe certain basic health rules to minimise the risk of infection. Allow yourself enough time to acclimatise and do not underestimate the strength of the sun's rays. Remember to pack suntan lotion (SPF 18 or more) and a sun hat. Air-conditioning is a mixed blessing due to the abrupt change from heat outside to fridge-like temperatures indoors. In most cases, fans are preferable.

Outside the major hotels eat only cooked or fried foods. Avoid tap water, salads, and unpeeled fruits. Bottled mineral water is widely available. Experienced travellers in the tropics never touch alcohol before sundown. Trying Balinese food is an essential part of the holiday experience and, as long as you observe the basic precautions, you should enjoy it.

Medicines are available

Bottled mineral water is widely available

Emergencies

Medical care in Indonesia is not yet up to Western standards. A private health insurance policy, including emergency transport back home if medically necessary, is strongly advisable. In case of serious illness, it's strongly recommended you fly to Singapore or Australia.

For minor ailments, go to the Surya Husada Clinic, Jalan P Serangan 1-3, Denpasar, tel: (0361) 233787. This private clinic specialises in the treatment of foreign tourists.

Emergency dental treatment can be obtained from Dr Indra Guizot, Jalan Pattimura 17, Denpasar, tel: (0361) 222445.

Clothing

Light cotton clothing is ideal. Don't pack too many clothes, as you won't be able to resist the items on sale throughout the island. If you plan excursions into mountainous regions, a warm pullover will be useful. A sun hat and an umbrella are useful accessories at any time of year.

Etiquette

Signs at temple entrances often indicate what is considered appropriate. No one may enter a temple without a waist sash. Buy one at the start of the visit and carry it with you if you plan to visit other temples, otherwise sarongs and sashes are usually available for rent at the entrances. Since blood defiles a temple, people with bleeding wounds and menstruating women may not enter. Their presence would necessitate a purification ceremony.

During ceremonies, *adat* clothing is desirable. This is the traditional festive clothing prescribed by the *adat*, the unwritten law, of the Balinese. When in doubt at temple ceremonies, do as the Balinese – kneel when they do so, and keep your head lower than that of the priest.

Nudity on the beach is impolite and illegal. Wear your bathing suit at the beach or the pool.

The head is considered holy, and even lovingly stroking a child's hair is regarded as an insult to dignity. Correspondingly low in the hierarchy come the feet, which should never be pointed or directed at anyone. Similarly taboo is the left hand: use your right for giving and receiving. Exchange of affection in public is not acceptable, and in temples forbidden. Begging is frowned upon, and you're advised not to give anything to begging children.

In an argument, avoid gesticulating loudly and making a scene – when in doubt, a smile can help to bridge linguistic and cultural barriers.

Heed the temple signs

ATTENTION

I. THOSE WHO ARE NOT ALLOWED TO ENTER THE TEMPLE ARE :
1. LADIES WHO ARE PREGNANT
2. LADIES WHOSE CHILDREN HAVE NOT GOT THE FIRST TEETH
3. CHILDREN WHOSE FIRST TEETH NOT FALLEN OUT YET
4. LADIES DURING THEIR PERIOD
5. DVOTEES GETTING IMPURE DUE TO DEATH
6. MAD LADIES /GENTLEMEN
7. THOSE NOT PROPERLY DRESSED
II. ALL DVOTEES ENTERING THE TEMPLE SKOULD MAINTAIN CLEANLINESS AND ENVIRONMENTAL CONSERVATION

Photography

Film can be readily purchased in Bali, although they are not always stored under ideal conditions.

Take along plenty of film as you travel the island, Bali offers a wealth of photographic opportunities. Don't forget the locals are not automatically suitable subjects. Exercise discretion, ask for permission before photographing individuals. Sign language is usually adequate. This is particularly important during religious festivals. Use of flash is forbidden during night ceremonies in temples.

Beachwear

Theft
Petty theft is becoming increasingly commonplace in the tourist centres. Leave expensive jewellery at home and keep valuables in the hotel safe.

Diplomatic representation
Australia: Jl. Prof. Moch. Yamin 4, Renon, Denpasar, tel: 235092, 235022, fax: 235146.
France (Honorary): Jl. Bypass Ngurah Rai 35, Sanur, tel/fax: 285485.
Germany (Honorary): Jl. Pantai Karang 17A, Sanur, tel: 288535, fax: 288836.
Italy (Honorary): Jl. Bypass Ngurah Rai 126G, Sanur, tel: 411562, fax: 289743.
Japan: Jl. Raya Puputan 170, Denpasar, tel:227628, fax: 231308.
Mexico (Honorary): PT Puri Astina Putra, Jl. Prof. Moch. Yamin 1A, Renon, Denpasar, tel: 223266, fax: 231740.
Netherlands (Honorary): KCB Travel, Jl. Raya Kuta 127, Kuta, tel: 751517, fax: 752777.
Norway and Denmark: Jl. Jayagiri VIII/10, Denpasar, tel: 235098, fax: 234834.
Sweden and Finland: Segara Village Hotel, Jl. Segara Ayu, Sanur, tel: 288407, fax: 287242.
Switzerland and Austria (Honorary): Swiss Restaurant, Jl. Pura Bagus Teruna (Jl. Rum Jungle), Legian Kelod, tel: 751735, fax: 754457.
United States: Jl. Hayam Wuruk 188, Renon, Denpasar, tel: 233605.

Glossary
Adat: Unwritten law based on tradition
Bale: Open pavilion in the courtyard of a temple
Banjar: District of a Balinese village which includes the married male members of the community
Meru: Shrine with multiple roofs derived from Mount Mahameru, the sacred mountain of Hinduism
Odalan: Balinese festival marking the anniversary of the dedication of a temple
Pura: Temple
Puri: Palace
Tirtha: Holy water
Trimurti: The Hindu trinity of Brahma, Shiva and Vishnu.

*Balinese luxury and
more basic accomodation*

Accommodation

If you want to enjoy real luxury in a Balinese setting, expect to spend at least US$300 or more a night. The good news, however, is that there is no need to sleep on the beach if you can't afford to fork out such huge sums. Clean and comfortable rooms can be had for much less. Soon after the completion of the 10-storey Grand Bali Beach Hotel at Sanur in the 1960s, a regulation was passed prohibiting the construction of buildings taller than palm trees. Architects also began to add local flavour to hotels by making use of local building techniques and materials. In many instances, tropical vegetation has helped to turn hotel complexes on Bali into miniature paradises.

There is a wide choice of accommodation on Bali. If you aren't too demanding, you will immediately feel at home in a *losmen*, a small guesthouse. As these are generally run by Balinese families, they offer the chance to establish contact with the local people. In the region around Ubud, many families earn extra income by letting out one or more rooms in their home to tourists. The rooms usually have a fan and a bathroom. In the most basic of *losmen*, the bathroom will be a *kamar mandi*, a traditional Indonesian bathroom with a squat toilet and a large tub of water with a scoop. You wash yourself outside the tub and pour water over yourself with the scoop. A *mandi* should not be confused with a bathtub, as the water must always be left clean and full for the next user.

During the low season, many hotels will negotiate prices. If you stay for a while, ask for a discount.

The following are hotel recommendations for the destinations covered in this book. They fall roughly into the following three price categories: $$$ = expensive; $$ = moderate; $ = inexpensive.

Bedugul (area code 0361)
$$$Bali Handara Kosaido Country Club, tel: (0362) 22646, fax: 23048.

Candidasa (area code 0363)
$$$Amankila, tel: 41333, fax: 41555. One of the three plush Aman resorts on the island, this one lies a few kilometres outside the village. It offers the very best of the best at correspondingly high prices (rooms at any of the Aman resorts are above US$500). **$$$Puri Bagus**, tel: 41292, fax: 41290. Attractive resort by the sea, frequently chosen by tour groups. **$$$The Watergarden**, tel: 41540, fax: 41164. Exclusive little complex away from the beach. The only choice in Candidasa for visitors in search of absolute peace and attractive surroundings. **$$Kubu Bungalows**, tel: 41256, fax: 41531. Enchanting location on the mountainside with accommodation in various price categories. **$$Puri Tinarella**, tel: 41373, fax: 41971. Attractive but inexpensive hotel complex on the edge of the village. **$Pondok Bamboo**, no tel. Central location, with beach. The best choice in the bottom-of-the range category. **$Geringsing**, no tel. Traditional *losmen* directly by the sea. Simple but clean and inexpensive.

Candi Kuning/Bedugul (area code 0368)
$Guesthouse Ashram, Candi Kuning, Bedugul, tel: 21450. Simple but unduly expensive rooms in a pretty location with views of Lake Bratan.

Denpasar (area code 0361)
$$Natour Bali Hotel, Jalan Veteran 3, tel: 225681, fax: 235347. Tourists no longer stay much in Denpasar, but mention should be made of this historic hotel which dates from colonial times.

Jimbaran (area code 0361)
$$$Bali Inter-Continental, Jalan Uluwatu, tel: 701888, fax: 701777. Set in 14 hectares (35 acres) of landscaped gardens with 425 rooms. Outstanding architecture with art works and sculpture. Faces a beautful white sandy beach. **$$$The Four Seasons**, Jalan Uluwatu, tel: 701010, fax: 701022. Built on a terraced hillside amidst beautiful gardens, this deluxe resort has 147 exquisite villas, each with a private splash pool. An ideal honeymoon getaway but expect to pay at least US$500 a night.

Kuta/Legian (area code 0361)
$$$The Oberoi, Legian Beach, Jalan Kaya Aya, tel: 730361, fax: 730791. A perfectly paradisiacal luxury bungalow complex on what is probably the loveliest beach on the island. The best address in Kuta/Legian and one of

99

A Balinese-style welcome

the best on the island. Rooms from US$225 up. **$$$Ramada Bintang Bali Resort**, Jalan Kartika, Kuta, tel: 753292, fax: 753288. Luxurious rooms and suites set in landscaped gardens with a private stretch of beach. Wide range of restaurants and facilities such as swimming pool, fitness centre, squash and tennis courts. **$$Poppies Cottages**, Gang Poppies I (Poppies Lane 1), Kuta, tel: 751059, fax: 752364. A classic amongst the typical local bungalow complexes; the same applies to the adjoining garden restaurant. Reservations recommended. **$$Legian Beach**, Jalan Melasti, Legian, tel: 751711/5, fax: 752652. Pleasant hotel for groups, directly on the beach and conveniently situated between Kuta and Legian. Suitable for families; excellent cuisine in the hotel restaurant. **$$Santika Beach Hotel**, Jalan Kartika Plaza, Kuta Beach, tel: 751267/9, fax: 751260. Situated on the outskirts of Kuta in a lovely garden. Reservations recommended. **$Asana Santhi Willy**, Jalan Tegalwangi 18, Kuta, tel: 752273, fax: 752641. Small, centrally located complex with comfortable rooms and a family atmosphere. Near the beach. **$Barong Cottages**, Jalan Gang Poppies II, Segara Batu Bolong, Kuta Beach, tel: 751804, fax: 751520. Small and extremely charming complex set in a garden with swimming pool.

Poppies Cottages

Hidden Paradise Cottages

Aditya Bungalows

Lovina Beach (area code 0362)
$$Banyualit Beach Inn, Lovina Beach, Kalibukbuk, tel: 41789, fax: 41563. Attractively furnished, ultra-clean rooms and bungalows and a friendly atmosphere. The restaurant is also recommended. **$$Palm Beach Hotel**, Lovina Beach, tel: 41775, fax: 41639. Spacious and well-kept rooms. Reservations recommended. **$$Sol Inn Lovina**, Lovina Beach, tel: 41265, 41285, fax: 41659. Modern bungalows in a pretty garden setting. Swimming pool. **$$Aditya Bungalows**, tel: 41059, fax: 41342. Bungalow complex in a quiet location. Good standard and attractive prices. **$Purnama Homestay**, Lovina Beach. Good value for money, comfortable accommodation and a welcoming atmosphere.

Pemuteran (area code 0362)
$$Pondok Sari Beach Bungalows, Pemuteran Grokgak, tel/fax: 92337. Tastefully decorated bungalows all in an idyllic setting. Restaurant.

Munduk (area code 0362)
$$Puri Lumbung, tel/fax: 92810. A pretty bungalow complex just inside the village limits.

Nusa Dua (area code 0361)
$$$Amanusa, tel: 772333, fax: 772335. A luxurious

oasis on the fringes of Nusa Dua. A true getaway for the idle rich. **$$$Grand Hyatt**, tel: 771234, fax: 772038. Huge hotel complex, surrounded by lush gardens and winding lagoons on a lovely beach. Suitable for families. **$$$Hilton International**, tel: 771112, fax: 771616. Tastefully built in the style of a water palace, this hotel features large and comfortable rooms.

The Grand Hyatt

Sambirenteng *(area code 0361)*
$$Alam Anda Bungalows, tel. and fax: 752296. This is an idyllic place to break your journey overnight. Under German management, this is a small hotel specialising in diving or water sports holidays. Contact Pike Travel in Kuta, tel: 752296

Sanur *(area code 0361)*
$$$Puri Santrian, Jalan Danau Tamblingan, tel: 288009, fax: 287101. Idyllic, well-designed hotel complex with bungalows directly on the beach. Reservations are recommended. **$$$Hotel Sanur Beach**, Jalan Danau Tamblingan, tel: 288011, fax: 287566. Beach hotel popular with tour groups and families alike; friendly staff. The best rooms are in the new wing. Reservation recommended. **$$Segara Village**, Jalan Segara Ayu, tel: 288407/8, fax: 287242. A jewel amongst the many hotels in Sanur; typical local bungalows and hotel complex near the beach. Children welcome. Reservations recommended. **$Villa Kesumasari**, Jalan Cemara 22, tel: 287492, fax: 288876. In a quiet location; inexpensive bungalows for individualists. **$Puri Mango Guesthouse**, Jalan Pantai Sindhu 15, tel: 288411, fax: 288598. Offers good value for money. Nice family atmosphere; swimming pool.

Toya Bungkah *(area code 0366)*
$Amertha's Restaurant & Bungalows, Jalan Penelokan. The place is simple, clean and attractively located by the lake. **$Lakeview Homestay**, Jalan Penelokan, tel: 51464. Basic rooms but spectacular views.

Tulamben *(Kubu Beach – area code 0363)*
$Paradise Palm Beach Bungalows. Simple bungalows with an attractive location directly on Kubu Beach itself. Diving courses available.

Ubud *(area code 0361)*
$$$Amandari, Kedewatan, tel: 975333, fax: 975335. The ultimate luxury resort – from its stunning location to its mega-sized rooms and its prices. Its spectacular pool appears to 'drop' into the valley below. **$$$Kupu Kupu Barong**, Kedewatan, tel: 975478, fax: 975079. A luxury complex that comes close, but not quite, to matching

Amandari Hotel

Ubud Homestay Bungalow
Opposite: beach at the Bali Hyatt

Amandari's standards. Has lovely rice terrace views. **$Dewi Sri Bungalows**, Jalan Hanoman 69, Padang Tegal, tel: 975300, fax: 975777. A jewel on the edge of the rice fields. **$$Pringga Juwita**, Jalan Bisma, Ubud, tel: 975734, fax: 975734. Central yet quiet location. Attractively furnished. **$$Hotel Tjampuhan**, Campuhan, tel: 975368, fax: 975137. Renowned hotel on a quiet hillside, breathtaking view over a river valley, swimming pool. Reservations recommended. **$$Ulun Ubud Cottages**, Sangingan, Ubud, tel: 975024, 975762, fax: 975524. A Balinese-style bungalow complex with attractive artistic details. The cottages are spacious and there are lovely views of the river. **$$Hotel Kokokan**, Jalan Pengosekan, Ubud, tel: 975742, fax: 975332. Luxury bungalows in a very quiet situation in the midst of a lovely tropical garden. Swimming pool. Reservations are recommended. **$Kubuku**, Monkey Forest Road, Ubud, fax: 975120. Simple and clean with nice family atmosphere; probably the best choice for all lovers of sunsets. **$Pande Permai Bungalows**, Monkey Forest Road, Ubud, tel/fax: 975436. Charming complex with comfortable rooms. Will appeal to thrifty travellers.

Lombok *(area code 0370)*
Gili Meno
$$Gazebo Meno Resort Cottages, Gili Meno; reservations in Mataram, Jalan Majapahit 1, tel: 35795.

Kuta
$Anda Bungalow & Restaurant, tel: 554836.
$Cockatoo, tel: 554830 and 554831.
   Both resorts are simple bungalow complexes, partly constructed in the style of *Sasak* rice barns..
$$Novotel, tel: 553333, fax: 553555.

Senggigi Beach
$$$Sheraton Senggigi Beach, Jalan Raya Senggigi, tel: 93333, fax: 93140. A magnificent beachfront complex with plenty of atmosphere. Both rooms and bungalows are available. **$$$Lombok Intan Laguna**, Jalan Raya Senggigi, tel: 93090, fax: 93185. Options in this luxury beach complex include standard rooms, bungalows, cottages and the Laguna Villa. **$$Puri Bunga Beach Cottages**, Senggigi, tel: 93353, fax: 93286. Fine views from the bungalows above the beach. **$$Melati Dua Cottages**, Jalan Raya Senggigi, tel: 93288, fax: 93028. Bungalows with typical local architecture. No swimming pool, but a friendly atmosphere. **$Pondok Senggigi**, Jalan Raya Senggigi, tel: 93275, fax: 93276. Immaculate, spacious bungalow complex with a casual atmosphere and live music several times a week.

The Lombok Intan Laguna

Index

Accommodation...**98–102**
Agriculture **7–8**
Air Panas,
  hot springs **62**
Air Sanih **54**
Alas Kedaton
  Monkey Forest.........**34**
Amlapura....................**50**
Ampenan **65**
art **73–5**

Bale Kembang............**45**
Bali Barat
  National Park...........**87**
Bali Museum **22**
Bangli **58**
Barong dance **37, 78**
Batubulan **36**
Bedugul **57**
Bedulu **41**
Bina Wisata
  Tourist Centre..........**26**
Bona **43**
Brahma Vihara
  Monastery......**56, 62**
Buddhism **9–11**
Bukit Badung
  Peninsula **23–4**
Bukit Jambal **45**

Cakranegara................**65**
Campuhan, walk to **28**
Candidasa...............**48–9**
Candi Kuning **57**
caste system **12–13**
Celuk **37**
Church of St Joseph ...**23**
climate..........................**7**
cockfighting **9, 69**
Craftsmen's Road....**36–7**
cremation....................**72**
Culik **54**

Dance **76–9**
Denpasar **22–3**
drink **82**

Economy...............**14–15**
Eka Das Rudra
  festival **47**
environment **7–8**
etiquette..................**96–7**

Fabrics **75**
festivals and
  ceremonies...........**71–2**
flora and fauna **8–9**
food **81–2**
foreign
  artists **25, 27–8, 74**

Galungan festival **71**
Gamelan **76**
Gedung Kirtya
  Library **55**
Gianyar.......................**43**
Gili Air........................**65**
Gili Meno **65**
Gili Trawangan **65**
Goa Gajah
  ('Elephant Cave') **42**
Goa Lawah
  ('Bat Cave')..............**49**
Gunung Agung......**46, 47**
Gunung
  Batukau............**34, 62**
Gunung Batur **60**
Gunung Kawi **39–40**
Gunung Rinjani **67**

Hiking and
  climbing...............**86–7**
Hindu epics **10, 76–7**
Hinduism.....................**9**
history **16–17**

Jewellery.....................**37**
Jimbaran Beach **24**

Kapal **32**
Karangasem
  dynasty **50**
Kecak dance **78**
Kerta Gosa
  (Court Hall) **44**
Klungkung...............**43–5**
Kotaraja......................**67**
kris......................**70, 75**
Kubutambahan **54**
Kuningan festival **71**
Kuta...................**20–1, 65**

Lake Bratan **57**
Lake Buyan **56**
Lake Tamblingan **56**
landscape..................**5–7**
language **13–14**
Legian **20–1**
Legong dance **78–9**
Lipah Beach **54**
Lombok.................**63–7**
Lombok Pottery
  Centre **67**
lontar books.........**52, 55**
Lovina Beach **56, 62**
Loyok **67**

Marga.........................**34**
marriage **72**
Mas.............................**37**
Mataram **65**

Mengwi **32**
Menjangan
  (Deer Island)............**57**
metalwork **75**
Monkey Forest **29**
Monkey Forest
  Road **28–9**
Munduk......................**56**
music **76**

Narmada.....................**66**
Neka Museum **27**
Nusa Dua................**21–2**
Nusa Lembongan **24**
Nusa Penida **24**
Nyepi festival **71**

Odalan festival............**71**
outriggers **54, 86**

Padang Bai..................**49**
painting **73–4**
Pasar Badung **23**
Pasar Kumbasari **23**
Pejeng....................**40–1**
Peliatan.......................**37**
Petulu..........................**38**
Penelokan **59–60**
Penestanan..................**28**
Penujak.......................**67**
Penulisan **61**
politics........................**15**
Pondok Sari **57**
prahus
  (outriggers) **54, 86**
puppeteers **33, 37**
Pupuan........................**62**
puputan.................**16–17**
Pura Beji.............**29, 55**
Pura Besakih **45–7**
Pura Dalem
  Padang Tegal **29**
Pura Dalem Sidan **58**
Pura Jagaraga **61**
Pura Jagatnata **22**
Pura Kehen.............**58–9**
Pura Lingsar................**66**
Pura Luhur
  Batukau...................**35**
Pura Meduwe
  Karang....................**54**
Pura Penataran Sasih...**41**
Pura Puseh
  Batubulan **36–7**
Pura Taman Ayun ...**32–3**
Pura Tanah Lot............**35**
Pura Tegeh Koripan....**61**
Pura Tirtha Empul.......**38**
Pura Ulu Watu............**24**
Pura Ulun Danu..........**57**

Puri Agung
  Kanginan **50**
Puri Lukisan
  Museum....................**27**
Puri Saren...................**28**
Puri Semarapura.........**44**
Puri Taman Mayura **65**
Puru Gunung Kawi **38**
Puru Meru **65**
Putung **48**

Rambitan....................**67**
religion **9–12**
restaurants **82–4**
rice
  terraces **34–5, 38, 53**

Sambirenteng **54**
Sangsit........................**55**
Sanur..........................**21**
Sasaks.........................**64**
Sawan.........................**61**
Sayan Valley **26, 85**
Semarapura see
  Klungkung
Senggigi Beach **64–5**
shopping.....................**94**
Singaraja **55**
stonemasonry **36–7, 73**
Sukarara......................**67**
Sukawati.....................**37**
Suranadi **66–7**
Sweta..........................**65**

Tabanan......................**35**
Tegallalang **38**
Temples..................**69–70**
Tenganan **51–2**
Tetebatu......................**67**
theatre.....................**76–9**
Tirtagangga **50–1**
tooth-filing
  ceremony **72**
Toya Bungkah.............**60**
Toyapakeh..................**24**
transportation **89–91**
Tulamben **54**

Ubud......................**25–9**
Ujung...................**50, 53**

Watersports............**85–6**
Wayang Kulit
  dance........................**77**
Werdhi Budaya
  Art Centre.................**23**
woodcarving....**37, 74–5**

Yeh Pulu.....................**42**
Young Artists **28, 74**